COOK THAI AT HOME

Authentic recipes with accessible ingredients

Sirilak Wichianpaisan (Salee)

Photography by Surasart Areear and Taran Wilkhu

The Big Cheeks Publishing

INTRODUCTION

Food has been an enormous part of my life since I was a child. I remember getting involved in the kitchen out of curiosity at a very young age. Everyone in my family is a fantastic cook: my mum, my dad, my sister - even my brother, who doesn't actually cook that often, not to mention a host of other relatives, including aunties, uncles, second cousins - and my grandma. I'm very fortunate to have plenty of happy childhood memories, most of which involve great food. Food brought my friends and family together: everyone contributing something, chatting together in the pandemonium of the kitchen - and overindulging - while the kids ran around until they dropped. One great thing about Thai cooking is that it's made for sharing; there's always enough if an unexpected guest turns up at your door in the middle of a meal (something very common and considered perfectly normal in Thailand).

Recent trips to my home town have brought me right back to my roots. Few tourists have heard of it - it's a place called Phitsanulok. It sits at the border where the bottom of the northern region and the upper part of central Thailand - a bit like the Midlands in the UK. It is a land of plenty; the city centre has a relatively strong economy and a good selection of schools and colleges, with a university. But most of the land is still used for farming and agriculture, which means a fantastic range of fresh local produce is always on hand at incredibly good value.

Phitsanulok railway station has been a centre for local trades for decades. It is the gateway to the north linking this part of the country to its capital and other regions.

6

Despite the parade of new trendy shops, restaurants and shopping centres that have been popping up in recent years, Phitsanulok still preserves traditional Thai cuisine, and most traders have their own speciality. The highlights of my trips home have always been eating at my favourite noodle bar, run by the same family for generations. Every single bowl of noodles tastes just as wonderful as I remember it tasting as a child, as does the freshly made spicy papaya salad, and sticky rice in a bamboo tub, which we ate by the busy streets before driving to the countryside to visit my relatives – trips that normally ended with massive feasts.

Among my all-time favourite things as a child were the markets, particularly the one my mum and I used to visit after school, to get some fresh ingredients for dinner. I loved it there, and still do: it has a warm, local feeling; the store traders know you as a regular and you know them. On my most recent trip there, I couldn't believe my eyes when I glanced at the butcher's stall: it was still in exactly the same spot it had occupied for nearly twenty years, and – amazingly – the couple who own it had hardly aged.

I could go on about my wonderful childhood experiences, but my point is this: 'food' to me is not just about eating. When you cook and share, not only are you making a tasty, nutritious meal, but without realising it you are also creating a beautiful living memory for your loved ones, exactly as my friends and family did for me.

I often hear people say that they *love* Thai food, but don't know how to cook it or where to get the ingredients. It's precisely for that reason that I've written this book – like you, I also love Thai food. I hope to share with you the joyful experiences I have had and to show you how to make these superb dishes, whatever your cooking ability.

Don't worry if there isn't an Asian or Thai supermarket near you. The good news is that cooking Thai food is easy, and so many general supermarkets now offer a fantastic range of Asian ingredients. I have listed some commonly available substitute ingredients that you can use to achieve amazingly authentic flavours without compromising on the results, on page 33.

I am not a chef by profession, just a working mother with a passion for cooking - and especially the food I grew up with. At home, a freshly cooked meal is on the family dining table most evenings and weekends. Making most of the recipes in this book takes no more time than heating up a ready meal in the oven or waiting for your takeaway to be delivered. Trust me – if I can do it, so can you.

'If more of us valued food and cheer and above hoarded gold, it would be a merrier world.'
– J.R.R. Tolkien

CONTENTS

RECIPE FINDER

All recipes in this book are naturally dairy free except for those marked with *D where the alternatives are provided. The recipes which contain gluten are marked with *G.

This is my grandma's kitchen where all the original dishes were produced using these few basic pieces of equipment. It hasn't changed for as long as I can remember.

HANDY IN THE PANTRY

For someone new to Thai cooking, it can seem like a major operation. But most people would be surprised to discover how easy it can be once you know the basics and have the basics. Like most Western kitchens, which are likely to have a few staples – mayonnaise, tomato ketchup, brown sauce, mustard, balsamic vinegar and so on – Thai kitchens have certain ingredients that can be used over and over. Here's a handy list of things to stock your 'Asian cupboard' with items that will allow you to make delicious Thai dishes day after day. At home, I have my stock ingredients, and then do my weekly shop at the local supermarket. These ingredients can increasingly be found at specialist Asian shops; you can also order many of them online, from Asian supermarkets, some larger supermarkets or other online stores.

COCONUT MILK

Kathi กะทิ

Coconut milk is the liquid derived from squeezing the grated flesh of a mature coconut. It plays a vital part in stamping a 'Thai' signature onto the national cuisine. Its subtle nutty flavour, creamy consistency and distinctive aroma give a real depth of flavour to both savoury dishes and desserts. In Thailand, people usually buy freshly grated coconut from the market and press it in a bowl of cool water by hand on the day of cooking. Since the freshly pressed milk is not pasteurised, it goes sour very quickly and should to be used within a few hours. Like the olive oil hierarchy, the first press is extra virgin: intensely creamy and flavourful. The more you press, the thinner the milk gets.

Tinned coconut milk is widely available at a reasonable price in general supermarkets and specialist Asian shops. I have found that the Thai and Malaysian brands are of better quality

FISH SAUCE

Nam pla น้ำปลา

Fish sauce is an essential element of Thai cooking. It is an amber-coloured liquid extracted during the fermentation of fish (in most cases anchovies) with sea salt. As well as being added to dishes during the cooking process, fish sauce is also used as a base for a dipping condiment that is prepared in many different ways in each region. Thai families serve *phrik nam pla* – chopped chillies in fish sauce – in a little ramekin as a standard table seasoning, just like salt and pepper on the Western tables. Although the sauce on its own has a strong fishy smell, it complements Thai dishes wonderfully when combined with other ingredients. Thai brands are generally best for obvious reasons, but most commercial brands are acceptable. Unless I am making a vegan meal, I would avoid using soy sauce as a substitute for fish sauce because it can change the flavour of the dish to a certain degree. If you are allergic to seafood or shellfish, a good alternative is to make your own seasoning from seaweeds such as wakame or kelp, which should be readily available in most health food shops and Japanese groceries, or online.

Try boiling 1 cup of seaweed with 6 cups of water and 2–3 tablespoons of sea salt for 30 minutes. Strain the liquid and store in an airtight bottle. It should keep for up to a month at room temperature or for up to three months in the fridge.

LIGHT (THIN) SOY SAUCE

Si io khao ซีอิ๊วขาว

This sauce is made from a fermented mixture of soya beans, flour and water. It gives dishes a salty flavour and is used in Chinese-influenced dishes such as stir-fries and soups. You can get it in your local supermarket, or even at some service stations. Soy sauce contains gluten due to the flour component, but gluten free versions are usually available in most health food shops.

DARK SOY SAUCE

Si io dam ซีอิ๊วดำ

Dark soy sauce is aged for much longer than light soy sauce, hence its much thicker and richer consistency. Thai dark soy sauce has a different flavour from its Chinese counterpart: slightly salty with a hint of caramel; the added sugar also makes it quite sweet. At home I use a Thai brand, mostly for its subtle sweetness and to add a wonderful golden brown colour to a dish. Use this condiment sparingly, though, and taste your dish before adding it, as it can make a dish taste over-seasoned.

OYSTER SAUCE

Nam man hoi น้ำมันหอย

Traditionally, oyster sauce is made by slowly simmering oysters in water until the juice caramelises into a thick, brown, intense sauce. Today, oyster sauces are usually made with a base of sugar and salt, thickened with corn starch; oyster extract or essence is then added to give flavour to the base sauce. The flavour of commercial oyster sauce, and the quality, varies greatly. Some brands are also more salty than others – I use the least salty one I can find, so that I can adjust the flavour of the dish to suit my taste. A vegan version made from mushrooms is also available.

PALM SUGAR

Nam tan pip น้ำตาลปีป

This distinctively rich and creamy sugar is made from the sweet, watery sap that drips from the cut flower buds of the palmyra palm tree, or sugar palm. The sap is boiled at a high temperature until caramelised. It is then whipped and dropped in lumps onto baking paper or cellophane, or into containers. Most palm sugar is still in fact produced at cottage industry scale, even today. So because it is not highly processed like caster sugar, the colour, consistency, flavour and degree of sweetness can vary from batch to batch depending on many factors, including the amount of rainwater the palm trees got during the harvest, even within the same brand. The palm sugar available in the UK generally comes in a plastic tub and is often rock-hard. To soften it, warm it in the microwave for 30 seconds and then stir in a little bit of water - although bear in mind this tends to increase the likelihood of spoilage, reducing its otherwise indefinite shelf life. Substitute with coconut sugar, light brown sugar or honey if you absolutely cannot find it.

ROASTED CHILLI PASTE

Nam phrik phao น้ำพริกเผา

This paste also known as chilli jam, is traditionally made from roasted red chillies, shallots, garlic, dried shrimps and vegetable oil, seasoned with palm sugar, tamarind sauce and salt. It is often added to *tom yum* soup and stir-fries. This delicious paste can also be used as a dip with Thai prawn crackers or raw vegetables. You can buy nam phrik phao online and from Asian supermarkets. Its flavour varies across different brands; the sweeter ones are more suitable for dipping than cooking.

SHRIMP PASTE

Ka pi กะปิ

Back in the old days, *ka pi* was just another way for fishermen in the south of Thailand to preserve the excess catch of the day. It is made from salted shrimps or krill, cured or fermented for several days, sometimes months, and then dried in the sun. The dried shrimps are then ground and compressed to a smooth paste, which amazingly will keep forever.

Ka pi is now an essential ingredient in many spicy dips and sauces, and, in fact, it is part of all Thai curry pastes.

Personally, I think it's a shame that many people outside Thailand avoid adding it to their cooking because of its strong fishy smell. *Ka pi* signifies Thai cuisine, adding the characteristic body and depth to our dishes. So if you want to get an authentic Thai flavour in your cooking, use it!

TAMARIND SAUCE

Nam ma kham piak นํ้ามะขามเปียก

Like fruits such as apples, there are a few different types of tamarind. Those for eating are pleasantly sweet yet gently sour, whereas the cooking variety is sharp and tangy. Both types look exactly the same, so make sure you read the label.

While readymade tamarind sauce can be bought just like tinned coconut milk, it is quite easy to make a bowl yourself, which will give you a complex sweet and sour paste. Traditionally, a handful of fresh tamarind fruit pods are peeled and soaked in a cup of warm water for a few minutes before being squeezed to release the flavour from the flesh. The mixture is then strained to remove the seeds and any lumps. The consistency should be thick to start with – you can always dilute it by adding more water later.

WHITE VINEGAR

Nam som sai chu นํ้าส้มสายชู

Most Thai households use distilled vinegar made from sugar cane, coconut or rice. These types of vinegar contain between 4 and 7 per cent acetic acid, giving them a hint of sweetness. Thai vinegar is used mainly to season sauces and to make pickles and condiments. If you cannot find Thai vinegar, diluted white wine or cider vinegar is an acceptable substitute.

YELLOW SOYBEAN PASTE

Tao chiao เต้าเจี้ยว

This paste is made from fermented yellow soybeans, salt and water. It is often used as an additional ingredient in modern Thai cuisine, particularly in stir-fries and dipping sauces.

TRADITIONAL HERBS AND SPICES

Thai herbs and spices are key ingredients in making this cuisine distinctive. Not only do they enhance the flavours of the other ingredients, but studies – such as ones carried out by Thailand's Kasesart University and Japan's Kyoto and Kinki Universities – show that many of them have added health benefits. They are also used in Thai traditional medicine (though please do not use them for medicinal purposes without consulting a health professional!).

If you live in a big city, chances are you'll be able to find the fresh versions of these ingredients quite easily as they are available in most Asian supermarkets, such as those in London's Chinatown or the Thai supermarkets in west London. Don't be daunted if you live outside London: the Chinese, Indian and Turkish grocery shops (among others) – and even some health food stores – that you find dotted around the high street usually have a little section that stocks these too. Many food retailers also offer them online.

On a number of occasions I've tried substitute ingredients, some of which have worked wonderfully, some not so well. To save you time, I've included after this section the substitutes to which a Thai mum would give the green light. To my delight, I've also noticed that the bigger supermarkets have started offering more and more varieties of these herbs and spices in recent years. So, familiarise yourself with them and be ready to impress yourself with your cooking skills!

CHILLIES

Phrik พริก

As a general rule, the smaller the chilli, the harder it hits you. For me, the colour - green or red - doesn't make much difference, except to the appearance of the dish (if you're making a green curry or a red curry, for example). The question I always get asked is, 'Which curry is hotter?' My answer is simple: curries can be as hot as you like. Many chefs are convinced that because green chillies are still young, they tend to be more vicious than the red ones. On the other side of the hotness battle are red chillies, which are ripe and therefore have a hint of sweetness and are less spicy. Believe me, just because they're older doesn't always mean they've lost their spicy edge. In Thailand, it's said that if you keep adding more and more chilli, of any sort, your ears will explode very quickly!

I tend to use green and red chillies interchangeably, partly depending on the colour I want the dish to be - though most of the time it really depends on what's left in my fridge. A common misconception is that the seeds are the hottest part of the chilli. In fact, the spiciest bit is actually the white pith that holds the seeds to the inside of the chilli. It contains the largest amount of *capsaicin*, the irritant that produces the burning sensation you get after eating chillies. So if you prefer your food to be milder, deseed and de-pith your chillies before using them and always remember not to touch your eyes afterwards. Rubbing your hands with some olive oil before handling chillies will prevent long-lasting stinging.

In Thailand, chillies are used as a hot herbal medicine to help stimulate the metabolism. Many pharmaceutical companies produce supplements that contain chilli extract for various purposes, such as treating fungal conditions, alleviating muscle aches and controlling body weight. (If you're considering taking these products, always consult your doctor or pharmacist first.)

Thai cooking uses a huge variety of chillies, of all sizes and levels of heat. For most dishes, however, if you have these three types you should be covered:

Bird's Eye Chillies Phrik khi nu suan พริกขี้หนูสวน

These small, thin, pungent chillies are sometimes called Thai chillies, but they come from Latin America, particularly Mexico. They certainly have the most memorable heat. They are one of the main ingredients used in Thai curry pastes, soups, salads and dipping sauces. They will keep for a couple of weeks in the fridge or several months in the freezer.

Long or Fresh Chillies Phrik chi fa พริกชี้ฟ้า

Commonly found in supermarkets, these chillies are much bigger than bird's eye chillies and come in sizes ranging from about 5 to 15 cm long. You can use long chillies instead of bird's eye chillies, but they have a much less intense flavour and are less fragrant. Store them as you would do with bird's eye chillies.

Dried Chillies Phrik haeng พริกแห้ง

These are bird's eye or long chillies that have been dried in the sun for a few days. You can also make your own dried chillies in the oven: wash the chillies and pat them dry, remove the stems and then lay them on a baking tray. Without adding any oil, cook the chillies on a low heat (approximately 150°C/Gas Mark 2) for two to three hours, depending on the size of the chillies you are using. The trick is to leave the oven door slightly open, to dehydrate rather than cook the chillies. I stick a wooden spoon between the door and the oven itself. Turn the chillies halfway through cooking. Choose ripe, red ones so that you get a nice rich colour when you're finished.

CORIANDER

Phak chi ผักชี

Coriander, known as *cilantro* in the USA, can be used to make an essential oil. It contains six types of acid and is rich in vitamins and minerals (including vitamin C).

Thais use the whole coriander plant in cooking: the leaves, the stem and the roots. In the West, the fresh stems and feathery leaves are used like parsley, as seasoning and a garnish. Coriander roots are my favourite part of the plant, as they have an intense musky and citrus-like favour. Sadly, however, most supermarkets remove the roots before packing. If you see fresh, bright green bunches of coriander with roots, grab a few, or buy a live coriander plant (most big supermarkets sell them). Coriander roots make a wonderful marinade. You can use the stalks and leaves as substitutes for the roots but you need to use at least double the quantity.

FINGERROOT

Kra chai กระชาย

Fingerroot's shape — a cluster of finger-like rhizomes with a thin, light brown skin — gives it the nickname 'Chinese ginger' or 'Chinese keys'. I don't think this herb is as well-known internationally as other southeast Asian spices, and it is less easy to get hold of. Fingerroot has an earthy, peppery and camphor-like taste and is a key ingredient in jungle curries, stir-fries and steamed dishes. It is available in most Asian supermarkets and can be stored in the same way as galangal and ginger. You can sometimes get fingerroot steeped in brine in glass jars, or frozen. Unfortunately, I haven't found a good substitute for it yet, so if you absolutely can't find it in any form, it's best to leave it out of a recipe

Like its fellow spices, fingerroot also has a variety of therapeutic properties. In Thailand, the juice is used to treat indigestion and to improve blood circulation. The whole rhizomes are sometimes fermented in strong Thai vodka to make a traditional alcoholic beverage drunk by some Thai men, particularly in rural areas.

GALANGAL

Kha ข่า

The galangal rhizome has a similar shape to ginger, but is harder with a denser texture. Despite being related to ginger, its slightly sweet, peppery and earthy flavour gives a different fragrance and taste to dishes. Most Thai curry pastes contain galangal as a basic ingredient. For some reason, many celebrity chefs substitute it by ginger, which I personally think is disastrous, because Thais regard them as two completely different spices. My suggestion would be to try powered galangal if you can't get it fresh, and for some dishes to skip it altogether. Fresh galangal can be stored in a plastic bag in the fridge for a few weeks or in the freezer for several months.

I have often seen galangal available in larger supermarkets and online. Herbalists consider the galangal root to be antispasmodic and antibacterial and recommend it for treating indigestion, loss of appetite and sea sickness.

GARLIC

Kra thiam, กระเทียม

Garlic is a fundamental component of most Thai dishes – nearly all the recipes in this book contain garlic in some way. Thai garlic is much smaller and more pungent than the garlic typically available in Western shops (although that's perfectly fine for Thai cooking too). It has a strong, distinctive smell but this rapidly gets milder when the garlic is heated.

People have been aware of the health benefits of garlic for centuries. During the First World War, surgeons used garlic juice as an antiseptic to treat battlefield wounds. Garlic makes for a delicious meal, but if you don't want its distinctive smell to linger on your breath, eating fruits such as oranges, lemons or apples can help. Not surprisingly, perhaps, raw mint is particularly effective.

GINGER

Khing ขิง

Ginger rhizomes are used widely in many countries around the world, and Thailand is no exception. Ginger is a hot spice used to flavour soups, salads, stir-fries and curries, as well as in pickles. Young ginger has a light, translucent skin and is juicy with a relatively mild taste. Mature ginger stems are more fibrous and pungent. Whether you use young or old ginger depends on your personal taste and how much heat you prefer. I usually choose young and firm ones as they keep for longer.

Practitioners of Thai traditional medicine encourage breastfeeding mothers to eat ginger in any form, as it is believed to enhance the production of breast milk. Check out my recipe for Chicken with Ginger and Spring Onion (p.88) for an easy and effective dish. I guarantee you'll like the result!

HOLY BASIL

Ka phrao กะเพรา

These pointed and slightly variegated leaves release a pungent fragrance when cooked at high temperatures that counteracts strongly flavoured meat or fish. This is why they're popular in stir-fries, and they feature heavily in street food dishes such as phat ka phrao.

Traditionally, holy basil leaves are a big part of Thais' daily lives, and because they grow so easily, they're a common sight in gardens. When I was a child, I used to love being sent out to pick a fresh bunch when dinner was being prepared. The leaves have diverse healing properties. Because of their strong aroma and astringent taste, they are seen as a kind of 'elixir of life' that promotes longevity. In Thai medicine, the leaves are used to treat indigestion and bloated feelings, and mothers with newborn babies treat colic by mixing two or three drops of basil juice into a tablespoon of breast milk.

KAFFIR LIME

Ma krut มะกรูด

The leaves of the kaffir lime are used extensively in Thai cuisine, in the same way as bay leaves are used in the West. Fresh kaffir lime leaves give off an amazingly refreshing aroma, and their spicy, lemony flavour brings a distinctive citrus touch to soups and curries. I have only ever seen them on sale in Asian shops, but you can buy kaffir lime trees online and from many garden centres, so why not grow a little one in your kitchen to ensure a ready supply? Frozen or dried leaves are also acceptable if you can't get fresh ones.

The fruit of the kaffir lime is rather bitter — only its zest is really used, mainly to flavour curry pastes. Thai people also use the refreshingly scented oil to achieve a similar effect to lemongrass in treatments like aromatherapy and oil massages, as it helps with relaxation.

LEMONGRASS

Ta khrai ตะไคร้

Lemongrass is a key ingredient of many well-known Thai dishes, such as *tom yum soup* and green curry paste. It is high in many vitamins and minerals, including vitamin A, calcium, phosphorus and iron. Although it is normally available in Asian markets, I have seen it increasingly on sale more and more in general supermarkets. Lemongrass is a fibrous and woody plant, and traditionally only the bottom 10-15 cm is used in cooking. Some chefs fish the chunky stalks out of the bowl before serving to make the dish easier to eat, as it's only the wonderful subtle and lemony fragrance that we're after. The upper part of the stalk is used as a natural mosquito repellent — varieties of the lemongrass plant are the source of citronella oil. Fresh lemongrass can be kept in the fridge for a few weeks, though I usually wrap it in cling film and freeze it on the day of purchase to maintain its freshness.

SHALLOTS

Ham daeng หอมแดง

This versatile and popular vegetable is a variety of onion.
Shallots vary in size but are typically about the same size as
a garlic bulb, with red or brown skins, and although they taste
a bit like onions, they're milder and slightly sweeter. Shallots
can be prepared in a variety of ways, one of which involves deep
frying them and serving as a condiment.

THAI SWEET BASIL

Ho ra pha โหระพา

Thai basil has small, narrow leaves, purple stems and purple-pink
flowers. The fragrant leaves have an aniseed or liquorice-like
flavour and are slightly spicy. Because these leaves are thicker
than holy basil, they're more stable at higher temperatures.
Thai basil is used in curries, stir-fries and soups, and the
fresh leaves can also be used to spice up salads.

You can usually find Thai basil in Asian supermarkets,
although if you don't shop at one regularly you may want to make
the most of what you've bought. After you've used the leaves,
trim off about half a centimetre from the bottom of the stalks
and put the pieces in a jar of water at room temperature. After
a few weeks, new shoots should appear, giving you more basil
for your next favourite dish!

SUGGESTED SUBSTITUTE INGREDIENTS

If you live miles away from Thailand, understandably getting fresh Thai ingredients can be challenging. Nonetheless, don't let that stop you from experiencing the amazing tastes. I have summarised a list of substitute ingredients which I use in my home cooking recipes on a regular basis so that you can create delicious food whenever you want, wherever you are. It is worth mentioning that sometimes it is better to omit some herbs rather than replacing with something else due to their unique flavours. They are also listed here.

White vinegar	White wine vinegar or cider vinegar diluted with water 1:1
Glass noodles	Rice vermicelli noodles
Palm sugar	Coconut sugar, light brown sugar or honey
Coconut milk	Whole milk or any alternative milk
Green papaya	Carrot or kohlrabi or raw swede
Green mango	Cooking apple or pineapple
Holy basil	Mediterranean basil
Galangal	It is better to omit it than to try to replace it with ginger. (They are NOT interchangeable)
Fingerroot	Simply omit it if you cannot find any
Shiitake mushrooms	Any seasonal mushrooms
Spring roll pastry	Filo pastry
Fish sauce	Light Soy sauce
Thai aubergine	Any other type of aubergine
Tapioca flour	Cornflour

NOODLES

It is believed that the use of noodles in Thai cuisine was influenced by Chinese merchants around the mid-seventeenth century, when foreign trading activity flooded into the bays of Siam. The locals were fascinated by the versatility of noodles and since then have made them their own.

RICE NOODLES

Sen Kuai Tiao เส้นก๋วยเตี๋ยว

Rice noodles are made from a mixture of rice flour and water, which is steamed in large trays to form enormous rice 'pancakes' before being cut into various sizes: fat noodles (*sen yai*, เส้นใหญ่), thin noodles (*sen lek*, เส้นเล็ก) and vermicelli noodles/fine noodles (*sen mi*, เส้นหมี่). Which one you choose is really a matter of personal preference. Most rice noodles available outside Thailand are dried and need soaking in water for about 20-25 minutes (or until soft) before using.

EGG NOODLES

Ba mi เส้นบะหมี่

These delicious noodles are wheat-based, with eggs added. They come in a variety of thicknesses and shapes, round or flat. You can find them quite easily these days in the express meal section of the supermarket. If you are using frozen noodles, thaw thoroughly. If using dried ones, soak them in water for about 10-15 minutes, until soft, before cooking.

GLASS NOODLES

Wun sen วุ้นเส้น

These wonderfully light noodles are sometimes called bean thread, crystal or cellophane noodles. Unlike their counterparts, these noodles are made from ground mung beans. Good-quality ones are naturally gluten free; however, many of the brands on the market do contain added starch, so please be cautious when buying if you have a sensitivity to gluten in case of cross-contamination during the manufacturing process. The noodles come dried, and need to be soaked in warm water for 5-10 minutes before use. They are usually much longer than other noodles, so cutting them with kitchen scissors to a shorter length will make handling them more manageable. Glass noodles are very fine and make a delightful fresh salad. They cook quickly - in only a few minutes once soaked - so take care not to overcook them.

RICE

People who lived in the area that is now Thailand had an intimate connection with rice. In Khon Kaen province in northeast Thailand, clay pots containing rice flakes have been found dating back more than 5,000 years.

Today rice is a central part of Thai society, particularly at the meal table. Unlike in the West, rice is the main dish in Thailand, and whatever you have with it is its companion. These side dishes are known as *kap khao*, which means 'with rice'.

Many different varieties of rice are eaten in Thailand, and the type depends on the region. Jasmine rice, a long-grain variety of fragrant or aromatic rice, is the most common type. It's safe to say I'm not a great fan of commercial pre-cooked or 'easy-cook' rice. These types are too hard and flavourless for Thai cookery. Cooking rice is very simple, but different people nevertheless have their own ways of cooking it.

My preferred method is relatively hassle-free. following my recipes should guarantee a perfect pot of fluffy rice every time. Cook your rice at the beginning of cooking any meal and let it stand, so that you have it ready once the rest of your meal is done. There are a vast variety of rice types in Thailand; here I have listed a few of those most commonly available in Asian and general supermarkets.

FRAGRANT THAI JASMINE RICE

Khao hom ma li ข้าวหอมมะลิ

This type of rice is a fundamental part of the Thai diet. It's normally boiled or steamed (or cooked using a combination of the two). Nowadays most people use rice cookers rather than the traditional clay pot on a wooden stove, although you can still find people using this method in some rural parts of Thailand.

The amount of water needed to achieve perfect rice is a question I'm often asked — it seems to be one of the great mysteries of cooking rice! When I was a child, my mother always said, 'As long as you add enough water so that it covers the rice by a depth of a joint of your index finger, you will get a pot of perfectly cooked rice.'

Since moving to the UK, I have not used a rice cooker, because it takes up too much space in my kitchen. I use a non-stick saucepan with a lid instead, which works fine. Rinsing the rice is a matter of preference. Many people, especially in Asia, rinse it to wash away any dust or impurities produced during the manufacturing process. Unless I've kept in the cupboard for a long time, I personally don't rinse rice, as washing can remove many of the vitamins and minerals. Imagine having to rinse your oats every time you made a bowl of porridge!

Prep time
5 mins

Cooking time
10 mins

Serves
4–6

2 cups jasmine rice
3 cups boiling water
Pinch of sea salt
(optional)

YOU WILL NEED
Medium-sized saucepan
with a tight-fitting lid

Put the rice in the saucepan with the freshly boiled water and a pinch of salt (if you're using it).

Stir gently a few times to separate the grains. This will help the rice to fluff up when it's done.

Cover the saucepan tightly with the lid, and cook on a medium heat for 10 minutes.

Turn off the heat but leave the lid on. Let the rice cook in the steam for another 10 minutes (without peeping!) before serving.

___ Top tip ___

It doesn't matter what size your cup is — the key is to get the proportion of rice to water right. Tea cups or mugs work perfectly for me.

BROWN RICE

Khao klong ข้าวกล้อง

Unmilled rice used to be served to prisoners because it was cheap. White jasmine rice, on the other hand, was seen as the best quality rice, because it looked pure and elegant. It was therefore eaten by wealthy families and monks and served to royalty. Nowadays, thanks to the promotion of its health benefits, brown rice, and rice of other colours, has become very popular; it also tends to be more expensive. Because brown rice is not as refined as jasmine rice, it is packed with nutrition and slightly crunchy, with a nutty flavour, although it will take longer to cook.

Prep time
5 mins

Cooking time
20 mins

Serves
4–6

2 cups brown rice
4 cups boiling water
Pinch of salt (optional)

YOU WILL NEED
Medium-sized saucepan
with a tight-fitting lid

Add the rice to the saucepan with the freshly boiled water and a pinch of salt (if using).

Stir gently a few times to separate the grains. This will help the rice to fluff up when it's done.

Cover the saucepan tightly and cook on a medium heat for 20 minutes (twice as long as for jasmine rice).

Turn off the heat but leave the lid on and let the rice cook in the steam for a further 10 minutes before serving.

Top tip

It doesn't matter what size your cup is – the key is to get the proportion of rice to water right.

STICKY (GLUTINOUS) RICE

Khao niao ข้าวเหนียว

Sticky rice or Glutinous rice comes in milled and unmilled forms. Raw milled glutinous rice is white and looks milkier than other types of rice. The unmilled type can give glutinous rice a purple or black colour. As the name suggests, glutinous rice is different from other types of rice because it gets sticky when cooked.

Glutinous rice is traditionally consumed in the northern and northeastern parts of Thailand, although nowadays you find it in most parts of the country. For some reason, white sticky rice is more popular for savoury dishes, while the purple and black type is used more for puddings.

Prep time
5 mins

Cooking time
20 mins

Serves
4–6

TO COOK IN MICROWAVE
2 cups glutinous rice
3 cups boiling water
Pinch of salt
(optional)

YOU WILL NEED
Microwavable bowl or container with a tight-fitting lid (you can also use cling film)

Add the rice to a bowl with half the freshly boiled water and a pinch of salt (if using). Stir gently a few times to separate the grains. Cover tightly with a lid. If you're using cling film, pierce a few holes in it with a fork to allow some of the steam to escape. Cook in a microwave on a high setting (approximately 900 watts) for 5 minutes.

Add the rest of the water and stir well with a fork to make sure the water is distributed evenly. Cook for a further 5 minutes, and then check the grains; cooked glutinous rice will be transparent. If some of the grains still look opaque, add a little more water and give it a quick stir before putting it back in the microwave for another 2 – 3 minutes.

Once the rice is cooked, remove from the microwave and leave to sit with the cover on for a further 10 minutes before serving.

This method of cooking doesn't require soaking.

Traditionally, sticky rice is soaked overnight to loosen the tight structure of the grains, before being cooked in a bamboo steamer. My grandma used to add a handful of jasmine flowers during this process to infuse the rice with a gentle but sophisticated fragrance. You can also add your favourite herb or spice, such as a chopped stalk of lemongrass or a stick of cinnamon

TO COOK IN STEAMER

2 cups glutinous rice

1 cup boiling water for steaming (or according to the instructions on your steamer)

Pinch of salt (optional)

YOU WILL NEED

A bamboo steamer (or any type of steamer)

a large piece of muslin cloth

Soak the rice overnight in cold water with a pinch of salt (if using). Drain it before cooking.

Add a little water to the steamer and bring to the boil. Line the steamer's container with a large piece of muslin cloth, then add the drained rice.

Cover the rice with the edges of the muslin cloth before closing the lid. Steam for 20 minutes, then check the rice, making sure all the grains look transparent.

If they don't, generously sprinkle cold water onto the rice, then carefully stir through and leave to steam for a further 10 minutes.

Remove from the heat and leave to stand with the lid on for 10–15 minutes. This will help the rice stay soft for longer.

SMALL DISHES AND SNACKS

Although many Thai restaurants outside Thailand will call these starters, these dishes are traditionally eaten as snacks. In Thailand, people snack and graze their way through the day – and that's on top of breakfast, lunch and dinner. Why wouldn't they, when there are so many food stalls open around the clock on every corner! Most of these snack foods are such incredibly good value that you don't even have to think twice before grabbing a bite. However, they are very easy to make at home, so I've picked some of the classic dishes here to get your mouth watering, and have given them a bit of my own twist. Serve them however and whenever you like.

CRISPY SQUID WITH GARLIC & PEPPER

Pla meuk thot khatiam ปลาหมึกทอดกระเทียมพริกไทย

This recipe is super-quick and easy but wonderfully effective. I usually keep a bag of squid in my freezer and then defrost it in the fridge the night before I want to cook this. The trick to getting the squid nice and crispy is to make sure the oil is smoking hot before you cook it. But be careful not to overcook the squid: two or three minutes is all you need for each batch. Enjoy with a seafood dipping sauce (see page 157 for recipe), with chilli sauce, or simply with a squeeze of lemon.

Prep time
5 mins

Cooking time
10 mins

Serves
4

500 g squid
5 garlic cloves, roughly chopped
½ tsp salt
½ tsp ground white or black pepper
4 tbsp cornflour
240 ml oil, for frying

Rinse the squid, and cut into 2½ cm pieces. Pat dry. Mix the squid with half the garlic and the salt and pepper, then sprinkle lightly with the flour.

Heat the oil in a small saucepan until smoking. Fry the squid in batches for no more than a couple of minutes; when cooked, remove the squid, draining any excess oil, and place it in a bowl.

Once all the pieces of squid are done, fry the remaining garlic in the deep-frying oil until golden brown (about 2 minutes), then remove using a slotted spoon. Pop it into the bowl on top of the squid.

FISH CURRY CUPCAKES

Ho mok pla ห่อหมกปลา

This delicious curry is supposed to be rather solid, with an almost custard-like texture, and is traditionally steamed in banana leaves. But I prefer to bake it instead, to create a gorgeous golden brown and slightly crispy top. The sliced cabbage should be steamed and patted dry before cooking to get rid of any excess juice, which will dilute the flavour of the curry. When cooking, you can use oven-proof ramekins, cups or foil cupcake cases in a suitable baking tray – or whatever you have in your cupboard. I usually make these in cupcake cases, because the size makes this dish perfect for nibbling at parties. These can be served hot or cool.

Prep time
15 mins

Cooking time
20 mins

Serves
4–6

400 g filleted fish (pink or white-fleshed fish; I use cod), diced into 1cm cubes
2 free-range eggs
240 ml coconut milk, divided
3 tbsp cornflour, divided
2 tbsp red curry paste
6 kaffir lime leaves, finely sliced (reserve some as garnish)
Large bunch Thai basil leaves
1 tbsp fish sauce
2 tsp caster sugar
Pinch of salt
Large handful of finely sliced white cabbage, steamed for 3 mins
1 fresh red chilli, finely sliced, for garnish

FOR THE CUPCAKES

Preheat the oven to 180ºC/Gas Mark 4. Beat the eggs in a mixing bowl. Add ¾ of the coconut milk (saving the rest for the topping), the curry paste and 2 tbsp of cornflour to the bowl and whisk until smooth. Add the lime leaves, the Thai basil, the fish sauce, sugar and salt, and mix through. Add the fish and gently stir the mixture well.

Lay a thin layer of steamed cabbage in the bottoms of cupcake cases or ramekins.
Spoon the fish mixture into the cases until they're each three-quarters full, leaving some room for them to rise. Bake in the oven for 20 minutes.

FOR THE TOPPING

In a small cup or bowl, mix the remaining 1 tbsp of cornflour with the remaining coconut milk until dissolved.

Cover loosely with cling film and microwave on low power for 1 minute. You can also heat the dissolved mixture in a small saucepan over a low heat for 2–3 minutes or until the sauce has thickened.

Spoon the coconut milk on top of the cooked cupcakes, and garnish with the kaffir lime leaves and chilli before serving.

CHICKEN SATAY

Kai sate ไก่สะเต๊ะ

This Indonesian-influenced marinated chicken has gained popularity all over Southeast Asia, and Thailand is no exception. The dish is cleverly served with an aromatic, sweet peanut sauce and cucumber relish (see page 158 for recipes) to cleanse the palate between bites. Most places in Thailand will serve the chicken with a few slices of lightly toasted white bread on the side, which I usually use to mop up the delicious dipping sauce at the end. You can also use any other meat of your choice with this recipe, such as pork, beef or lamb. If you choose to use one of these, add a few tablespoons of pineapple juice or a teaspoon of whisky to the marinating sauce to tenderise the meat.

Prep time
10 mins

Cooking time
20 mins

Serves
4–6

Top tip

Don't forget to soak the wooden skewers in water for about half an hour before threading the chicken on, so that they don't burn when grilling.

600 g chicken breasts, sliced lengthways into thin pieces about 8 cm long
250 ml coconut milk
2 garlic cloves, crushed
2 tbsp light-flavoured oil
1 tbsp palm sugar
1 tsp ground coriander
1 tsp ground cumin
1 tsp ground turmeric
1 tsp salt
1 pack wooden skewers

In a large bowl, mix all the ingredients together. Cover and leave to marinate in the fridge for at least 2 hours, or overnight for the best results.

Thread the chicken slices onto the skewers. In a small saucepan, heat the remaining marinating sauce until boiling, then switch off the heat.

Grill the chicken, cooking it over a barbecue or under the grill on a medium heat. Baste the chicken occasionally with the marinating sauce, and turn the meat every 5 minutes or so until it's cooked and no pink flesh remains (about 20 minutes in total).

THAI PRAWN CAKES

Thot man kung ทอดมันกุ้ง

These moreish little cakes are my twist on the classic Thai fishcakes. They make a perfect starter for dinner parties, or nibbles to have with your favourite summer drinks. I use Japanese panko breadcrumbs – which you can now easily get from many shops and supermarkets – for a nice, flaky finish, but any other type of breadcrumb would also do. Remember, the fresher the prawns, the tastier the cakes.

These cakes are most delicious when deep-fried, but you can also bake them in an oven. Serve hot with the special dipping sauce or sweet chilli sauce. If you freeze these, they'll keep for up to six months.

Prep time
15 mins

Cooking time
30–45 mins

Makes
24 medium cakes

FOR THE CAKES

700 g fresh raw prawns, cleaned and peeled
Handful of coriander roots or coriander stalks, coarsely chopped
2 garlic cloves, crushed
2 tbsp cornflour
2 tbsp caster sugar
2 tbsp light soy sauce
1 tbsp oyster sauce or 2 tsp salt
1 tsp ground white pepper
100 g pork fat or lard (optional)
80 g plain flour
3 free-range eggs, beaten
150 g breadcrumbs
200 ml oil, for frying

FOR THE DIPPING SAUCE

4 tbsp sweet chilli sauce
4 tbsp water
1 tbsp fish sauce
2 tsp lime juice
Cucumber, finely chopped
Roasted unsalted peanuts, finely chopped
Coriander, for garnish

If you are going to bake your fishcakes, preheat the oven to 200ºC/Gas Mark 6.

In a food processor or blender, put the prawns, coriander root, garlic, cornflour, sugar, soy sauce, oyster sauce and white pepper, and the pork fat or lard if using. Blend the ingredients for a few minutes or until the texture is smooth. Transfer the mixture to a mixing bowl, and massage the paste well by hand for 5 minutes, or until the dough is sticky and puffy. Rest the mixture in the fridge for 30 minutes to an hour.

Once rested, shape the mixture into small balls each about 4 cm in diameter, then flatten them into a small patty-type shape. Wetting your hands with water will help prevent the mixture from sticking to your hands – I keep a small bowl of water on the side for this purpose when I make this dish.

Put the plain flour, beaten eggs and breadcrumbs each into a separate bowl. Dip each cake into the flour, then into the eggs; finally, coat it with breadcrumbs. Press the patty gently but firmly to ensure an even coating of breadcrumbs on all areas.

Heat the oil in a frying pan on a low heat, and then fry the prawn cakes for 2–3 minutes each side. Continue turning them and cooking until they are golden brown. If baking your fishcakes instead, brush them generously with vegetable or olive oil and then cook in the oven for 15–20 minutes. Mix all the dipping sauce ingredients together in a bowl and serve alongside the finished cakes.

SPRING ROLLS

Popia thot ปอเปี๊ยะทอด

When I was a kid, cooking spring rolls was one of my favourite weekend family activities. My mum or papa would cook the filling in a wok. My sister and I were in the wrapping department. I felt pretty proud of myself, eating something I'd crafted. Now my daughter loves doing the same with me.

Spring rolls are much easier to make than many people think. If you can't find the readymade Asian spring roll wrappers, you can use filo pastry instead. Keep the sheets that aren't being used covered under a damp cloth or kitchen towel, otherwise they will dry out and quickly start to crack. The same goes for the glass noodles: you can substitute these with the ready-cooked rice noodles that are available in the chiller cabinet at larger supermarkets, or cook your own rice vermicelli.

Traditionally, Thai spring rolls are deep-fried, but you can also bake them. I actually prefer this method most of the time, as it gives me time to put my feet up and have a cup of tea while they're cooking.

Prep time
45 mins

Cooking time
25 mins

Makes
20–24 medium rolls

330 ml light-flavoured oil, divided
150 g minced pork (or chicken)
2 garlic cloves, crushed
50 g glass noodles, soaked in room-temperature water for 20 mins (substitute 200 g ready-cooked rice noodles)
120 g white cabbage, finely shredded or roughly grated

PREPARING THE FILLING

In a wok or large frying pan, heat 2 tbsp of oil for 30 seconds. Add the garlic and the pork, and stir until the pork is cooked through.

Add the glass noodles or vermicelli, cabbage, mushrooms and carrot to the pan, and stir for a further 2–3 minutes.

Season with the fish sauce, soy sauce, oyster sauce and a pinch of white pepper. Transfer the filling into a bowl and set aside until it cools. If baking your spring rolls, preheat the oven at this point, to 200ºC/Gas Mark 6.

CONTINUED…

10-12 dried shiitake mushrooms,
soaked in water for 20 mins (substitute 30 g any other mushrooms)
1 medium-size carrot, grated
1 tbsp fish sauce
1 tbsp light soy sauce
1 tbsp oyster sauce
½ tsp caster sugar
A pinch of ground white pepper

YOU WILL NEED

24 frozen spring roll wrappers
(15×15 cm), thawed and kept
covered with a damp kitchen towel
Small bowl of water

PREPARING THE WRAPPERS

Lay a sheet of spring roll pastry on a clean
chopping board. Place 1-2 tbsp of the filling
mixture in the centre of each wrapper. Be careful
not to put too much filling in as the rolls will
burst.

Roll the wrapper around the mixture tightly.
Fold the edges inward to close. Moisten fingers
in a small bowl of water and brush the seams to
seal (like sealing an envelope). Repeat the
process until you have used up the mixture.

TO COOK

Heat the remaining oil in a wok until hot.
Carefully fry the spring rolls approximately 10
rolls at a time, until crispy and golden brown.

If baking the rolls, add 100 ml vegetable or
olive oil to a baking tray and place in the
preheated oven for about 5 minutes or until the
oil is very hot.

Take the tray out, carefully place the
spring rolls onto the tray, and brush them
generously with the hot oil.

Bake for 20-25 minutes or until golden brown
(add 10-15 minutes to the cooking time if you are
cooking from frozen). Serve hot with a small bowl
of sweet chilli dipping sauce.

THAI FISH CAKES

Thot man pla ทอดมันปลา

This classic dish is loved by everyone. In fact, these fishcakes are so delicious, it's worth doubling up on the quantities when you make them so that you can freeze the spares for a rainy day. I use 2 tablespoons of red chilli paste in this recipe, which is enough to get your taste buds dancing. You can always reduce or increase the quantity to adjust the heat to your taste.

Traditionally, these are deep-fried in a wok, but you can also cook them in an oven; they may not stay puffy for as long but it works just fine. A tip: have a small bowl of water on the side to wet your hands when making the cakes: this helps prevent the sloppy mixture from sticking to your hands. Serve these hot accompanied by cucumber relish (see page 158 for recipe).

Prep time
5 mins

Cooking time
30 mins

Serves
4–6

700 g skinless white fish
1 large free-range egg
2 tbsp red curry paste
1 tbsp tapioca flour or cornflour
1 tsp caster sugar
1 tsp oyster sauce or 2 tsp salt
120 g raw green beans, finely sliced
3 tbsp fresh kaffir lime leaves, finely chopped
1 tbsp fish sauce
500 ml oil, for frying

Combine the fish, egg, tapioca flour, sugar, oyster sauce and red curry paste in a food processor and blend for about 2–3 minutes, or until you get a smooth and sticky consistency.

Test the flavour by scooping a teaspoon of the mixture into a small ramekin and cooking it in a microwave for 15–20 seconds on medium power. Adjust the seasoning to taste. Transfer the mixture into a bowl, cover, and put in the fridge for 30 minutes.

Remove the paste from the fridge. If baking instead of frying, preheat your oven at this point to 200°C/Gas Mark 6. Fold the beans and kaffir lime leaves into the fish mixture.

Dampen your hands with water and, taking 2 tablespoons of the mixture at a time, form it into small patties about 5–8 cm in diameter. Repeat until you have used up all the fishcake mixture.

If baking the fishcakes, lay them on a baking tray, brush them generously with vegetable or olive oil, and then cook in the oven for 20–25 minutes. Otherwise, in a wok or a deep saucepan, heat the oil over a high heat until smoking hot.

Deep-fry the cakes for about 30–40 seconds each side until the cakes have puffed up and are golden brown.

SOUPS

A wide variety of soups can be found around Thailand, and each one has its own character, ranging from comforting, creamy coconut milk-based soups that hug you from the inside, to the spicy and tangy tom yum soup that switches on your taste buds, to light, clean broths that put you in a relaxed mood. Some of the combinations of herbs and spices in these soups can be similar, yet you can create a vast variety of soups by adjusting the quantity of ingredients and seasoning.

Thai cooking is ultimately down to personal preference: you can add or use more or less seasoning to your taste. In these recipes, the measurements I give are for how I like to make these dishes. But trust yourself, get cooking and have fun with it. Although many Thai restaurants outside Thailand often place the soups in the starter section, these soups are served as part of a main meal together with hot steamed rice.

CREAMY KING PRAWN TOM YUM SOUP

Tom yum kung nam khon ต้มยำกุ้งน้ำข้น

This tangy soup is perhaps Thailand's signature dish: its combination of Thai herbs gives it a beautiful, distinctive fragrance. To simplify the cooking process, I use chicken stock as a base for the soup, but if you can get hold of whole raw prawns with their shells and heads, make the most of them by making a stock from them. Boil the shells and heads in a pot of salted water for ten to fifteen minutes until you see a few drops of oil floating on the top. Strain the liquid and use it as your base; it'll give the soup a lovely rich prawn flavour. The lemongrass, lime leaves and galangal are edible, but not many people eat them as they are tough to chew, so you might like to fish them out before serving. Most Thai people use evaporated milk from a can or fresh milk for this soup. Serve as part of a main meal alongside steamed rice, or as a starter.

Prep time
10 mins

Cooking time
20 mins

Serves
4–6

800 ml homemade or readymade chicken stock
5–7 kaffir lime leaves, finely chopped
2 stalks lemongrass, cut into 2.5 cm-long pieces
½ stem galangal, finely sliced
400 g raw prawns, deveined
250 ml evaporated or whole milk or coconut milk
100 g oyster mushrooms (or any white mushrooms), cut in half
50 g cherry tomatoes
3–4 tbsp fish sauce
2 fresh bird's eye chillies (deseeded, coarsely chopped)
1 tbsp caster sugar
1 tbsp chilli paste (optional)
3–4 tbsp lime juice

Heat the stock in a deep saucepan over high heat until it starts to bubble. Add the kaffir lime leaves, lemongrass and galangal and bring to the boil. Reduce the heat to medium and simmer for 10 minutes, to extract the aroma of the herbs. After 10 minutes, remove the herbs from the pot if preferred.

Add the prawns, mushrooms and tomatoes towards the end of cooking, and add the milk last, to avoid separation. Season with the fish sauce, fresh chillies, sugar and chilli paste (if you're using it).

Squeeze the lime juice into a separate bowl rather than directly into the cooking pan. Turn off the heat before adding the lime juice and adjust the seasoning to taste. Serve, garnished with coriander.

CLEAR MUSHROOM TOM YUM SOUP

Tom yum het   ต้มยำเห็ด

This spicy, clear broth soup is rich with flavour and so refreshing. The aroma of lemongrass, galangal and kaffir lime will make your kitchen smell like a festival. The lemongrass, lime leaves and galangal are edible, but they're tough to chew; you can either fish them out before serving or leave them in the bowl for decoration.

Prep time
10 mins

Cooking time
20 mins

Serves
4-6

Top tip

Squeeze the lime juice into a separate bowl rather than directly into the cooking pan, then add it to the pot at the last minute, to avoid cooking the juice as well as avoiding the bitterness from the lime zest.

1 l chicken stock, vegetable stock or water
5-7 kaffir lime leaves, finely chopped
2 stalks lemongrass, cut into 2.5cm long pieces
½ stem galangal, finely sliced
200 g white mushrooms, cut in half (or whole button mushrooms)
50 g cherry tomatoes
3-4 tbsp fish sauce
(Optional) 2-3 fresh bird's eye chillies, or 1 tsp dried chilli
1 tsp caster or brown sugar
3-4 tbsp lime juice
Handful of fresh coriander

Heat the chicken stock in a deep saucepan over high heat until it starts to bubble. Add the lime leaves, lemongrass and galangal and bring to the boil. Reduce the heat to medium and simmer for 10 minutes, to extract the aroma of the herbs. After 10 minutes, remove the herbs from the pot if preferred.

Add the mushrooms and tomatoes. Season with the fish sauce and sugar, and fresh chillies if using.

Turn off the heat before adding the lime juice and adjust seasoning to taste. Serve, garnished with coriander.

AROMATIC COCONUT SOUP WITH CHICKEN

Tom kha kai ต้มข่าไก่

This rich and aromatic soup has almost the same list of ingredients as *tom yum* soup. Its vastly different taste, however, reflects just how versatile Thai cooking can be simply by adjusting the quantities of its key ingredients. Because of the amount of coconut milk used, *tom kha kai* is creamier and has a milder and more delicate taste than *tom yum*, but it is still packed with intense flavour, making it easy to enjoy for people of all ages. Most people in rural parts of Thailand use free-range chicken on the bone and add hard-boiled chicken blood to this soup. I use chicken breast fillets instead and have omitted the chicken blood to simplify the recipe. The lemongrass, lime leaves and galangal are edible, but they are tough to chew, so you might like to fish them out, although leaving them adds an extra infusion of herbal flavour. Serve hot as part of a main meal with steamed rice or as a starter for a more formal dining style.

Prep time
10 mins

Cooking time
20 mins

Serves
4–6

600 ml chicken stock or water
8–10 kaffir lime leaves, halved
1 medium stem galangal, sliced into 0.5cm thick pieces
3 stalks lemongrass, crushed with the flat of a heavy knife and cut into 2.5 cm long pieces
400 ml (1 can) coconut milk
4 chicken breast fillets, finely sliced
200 g oyster mushrooms, halved
100 g cherry tomatoes, halved
2 fresh bird's eye chillies (optional)
1 spring onion, cut into 2.5cm long pieces
5–6 tbsp fish sauce
½ tbsp palm sugar
4–5 tbsp lime juice
Handful of coriander, roughly chopped

In a saucepan, combine the stock or water, lime leaves, galangal and lemongrass. Bring to the boil, and keep at a rolling boil for about 5 minutes. Reduce the heat to low before adding the thinner liquid from the coconut milk, and leave to simmer for about 5 minutes. If your coconut milk is already mixed and you cannot separate the cream, add half the can now and the other half later. Remove the herbs from the pot at this stage if preferred.

Next add the chicken, and bring the soup back to the boil for about 5 minutes. Use a big spoon to remove any scum that floats to the top of the soup.

Add the mushrooms, tomatoes and chillies (if you're using them), and the creamy liquid from the coconut milk (coconut milk can separate if the cream is added too early). Leave to cook over medium heat for a further 2–3 minutes.

Add the spring onion and then season with the fish sauce and sugar. Turn off the heat, and add the lime juice. Check the seasoning and adjust if needed. Garnish with coriander before serving.

MINCED PORK PARCELS IN CLEAR BROTH

Tom chuet mu sup   ต้มจืดหมูสับ

This light, nutritious and tasty dish is perfect for the whole family, so I've designed the recipe to serve an average-sized family. I use the Chinese cabbage leaves to wrap the minced pork into little parcels, to make it more fun and to encourage my kids to eat more vegetables. If you just fancy something quick and easy, you can simply cut the leaves and drop them into the soup with the minced pork and the other ingredients.

The list of ingredients might look a bit long, but chances are you'll already have most of them in your cupboard, and it's actually a simple, un-fussy dish.

Prep time
30 mins

Cooking time
15 mins

Serves
4-6

FOR THE PORK PARCELS

1 large Chinese (napa) cabbage
20 spring onions, roots and bulb removed (use only the green parts)
400 g minced pork
2 garlic cloves, crushed
1 tbsp light soy sauce
1 tbsp fish sauce
1 tbsp oyster sauce
Pinch of ground white pepper

FOR THE BROTH

1 l pork stock (cubes are fine)
1 medium carrot, finely sliced into discs
5 coriander roots
2-3 tbsp light soy sauce
2-3 tbsp fish sauce
2 tsp caster sugar
4 tbsp light-flavoured oil, divided
3 cloves of garlic, crushed
Handful of coriander leaves for garnish (optional)

PREPARING THE PORK PARCELS

Cut the bottom 2.5 cm or so off the bottom of the Chinese cabbage, to separate the leaves. You need about 20 leaves, plus a few spares. Choose the longest leaves for this, if you can, as there will be more area with which to roll.

Place the cabbage leaves and spring onions on a plate together, sprinkle with a little water, and cook in a microwave on a medium heat (approx. 800W) for 1-2 minutes, to soften the leaves.

Put the minced pork into a bowl with the crushed garlic, soy sauce, fish sauce, oyster sauce and ground pepper, and mix well.

Add about 2 tablespoons of the mix in the middle of a cabbage leaf, and use a spring onion strip to tie the parcel with a knot. Repeat the process until you've used up the pork mixture, and then set aside.

PREPARING THE BROTH

Put the pork stock, carrot and coriander roots into a medium-size saucepan. Carefully add the pre-prepared parcels to the soup and cook over high heat until bubbling. Add the soy sauce, fish sauce and sugar, turn down the heat, and let it simmer for about 10 minutes.

While the soup is simmering, shallow fry the crushed garlic in 2 tablespoons of oil for 2-3 minutes, until golden brown. After 10 minutes, add the crispy garlic to the soup.

Sprinkle the bowls with the coriander leaves before serving.

CLASSIC RELISHES

Most Thai relishes contain chilli. As I explained in the Traditional Herbs and Spices section, there are many different varieties, which makes each dish versatile. If heat is not your best friend, you can substitute red or green bell peppers for the fresh or dried chillies instead. Make sure you deseed the chillies and remove any white membrane before cooking, so that you don't get the bitter flavour they can impart.

In Thailand, relishes are served as dips, with an assortment of fresh leaves and steamed vegetables, to accompany rice. I love them with a Thai omelette (see page 116 for recipe) or soft-boiled eggs, or just mixed with rice for a simple and delicious meal. They are so easy to make, especially if you have a food processor, and you can also freeze them as you would curry pastes. Try showing off at a barbecue party by serving one of these as a dip with cucumber and carrot sticks – you'll impress your lucky guests.

My great-grandmother sadly passed away a few years ago – but to be fair she lived until she was 105 years old! She spent more than eight decades of her long life as a very well-respected Thai traditional physiotherapist, helping people to get back on their feet. Dishes such as these are what she ate throughout her life. She must have been doing something right.

SWEET TOMATOES AND MINCED PORK RELISH

Nam phrik ong น้ำพริกอ่อง

This delicious sweet and sour relish originated in the north of Thailand but has become popular throughout the country. If you prefer a milder taste, deseed the chillies and soak them in warm water for a few minutes before you use them, which will dilute their heat. Like other Thai relishes, this is usually eaten warm with steamed vegetables, fresh lettuce, crispy pork crackling and hot sticky rice.

Prep time
10 mins

Cooking time
15 mins

Serves
4 as a sharing dip

Top tip

The secret of this dish is to use the best quality tomatoes you can find, and ones that are a little under-ripe, so you get a slightly sour flavour.

10 dried long red chillies, deseeded

4 shallots, peeled

6 garlic cloves

1 stalk lemongrass, finely chopped

Coriander roots from a bunch of coriander, plus a handful of stalks and leaves for garnish

Pinch of salt

4 tbsp light-flavoured oil

400 g minced pork

400 g fresh tomatoes, chopped

240 ml pork or chicken stock

½ tsp shrimp paste (optional)

2-3 tbsp fish sauce

2-3 tbsp tamarind sauce

1 tbsp palm sugar

Pound the dried chillies, shallots, garlic, lemongrass, coriander root and a pinch of salt in a pestle and mortar for a few minutes until the ingredients form a rough paste. In a large frying pan, fry the mixture in the oil for 2-3 minutes over medium heat. Add the pork and keep stirring.

After a few minutes, when the pork is about half-cooked, add the tomatoes, stock and shrimp paste (if you're using it). Continue cooking gently, stirring constantly, for another 5 minutes.

Add the fish sauce, tamarind sauce and sugar, stir well, and cook for a few more minutes. Transfer to a serving bowl, and garnish with the coriander before serving.

CHARGRILLED CHILLI AND MACKEREL RELISH

Nam phrik pla thu น้ำพริกปลาทู

This is a classic relish, commonly found on sale in markets as well as in most households. Not only is it easy to make, it's also light and highly nutritious. I make it the traditional Thai way, using a pestle and mortar. Don't worry if you don't have one though, as a food processor will do the job fine. Simply blend the ingredients together on a low setting to get a chunky, rough finish rather like guacamole.

This dish is typically made with long green chillies but there is no harm in using long red ones. You can also substitute half the chillies with bell peppers for a milder taste. Thais serve this cold as a main dish alongside soft-boiled eggs, vegetables such as steamed or raw Chinese cabbage leaves, fresh cucumber and raw or steamed Thai aubergines (which are about the size of golf balls and pale green in colour), and eat it with hot steamed jasmine rice.

Prep time
15–20 mins

Cooking time
10 mins

Serves
4 as a sharing dip

1 medium raw whole mackerel or two fillets, cleaned
4 shallots, peeled and cut in half
7–8 green chillies
4–5 garlic cloves, peeled
3 tbsp boiled water, cooled
3 tbsp fish sauce
2 tbsp lime juice
1 tsp caster sugar

Grill the mackerel under a medium grill or on a griddle pan for about 5 minutes each side, and then leave to cool down.

While the fish is cooking, toss the shallots, chillies and garlic in a dry non-stick pan over a low heat, stirring constantly, for 5–6 minutes or until they are soft and have started to turn brown. Transfer them to a pestle and mortar and pound for a few minutes, or blitz in a food processor on a low setting, until the mixture forms a rough paste.

Flake the mackerel from the bone, taking care not to leave any bones in the meat.
Add the mackerel to the mortar (or food processor) and pound together until all the ingredients are roughly mashed. Add a little water, and season the mix with the fish sauce, lime juice and sugar. Transfer the mix to a serving bowl.

NORTHERN-STYLE CHARGRILLED CHILLI RELISH

Nam phrik num น้ำพริกหนุ่ม

This particular relish is originally from the ancient Lanna Kingdom in the north of Thailand, although it's also popular in central and northeastern parts of the country. Different local tastes mean there are a few twists and variations you can make on the basic recipe, like adding fermented fish (*pla ra*), shrimp paste (*ka pi*) or lime juice. For this recipe, I'm sticking to the original Chiang Mai style, which is a mellower version. You can also toss all the raw ingredients in a clean wok for five minutes instead of putting them under the grill. This dish is typically made with long green chillies. This delicious dip is served cold and is usually accompanied by crispy pork crackling, fresh vegetables and a bamboo tub of hot sticky rice for sharing.

Prep time
10 mins

Cooking time
10 mins

Serves
4 as a sharing dip

Top tip

Substitute half or all the chillies with green bell peppers for a milder taste.

12-15 long green chillies, deseeded if you prefer a milder flavour
8 red shallots, peeled and cut into quarters
5 garlic cloves
Pinch of salt
2 tbsp boiled water, cooled
2-3 tbsp fish sauce
1 tbsp fermented anchovies (*pla raa*; optional)
1 tsp caster sugar
1 tbsp chopped spring onion
1 tbsp coriander leaves

Grill the chillies, shallots and garlic for 5-7 minutes or until they turn golden, or toss the ingredients in a dry, clean wok for 5 minutes over a low heat. Let them cool before peeling off any burnt skin.

Transfer the mixture into a pestle and mortar or food processor, and pound/blitz moderately with a pinch of salt for 5 minutes until it becomes a purée. Add a little water if it's too dry, but be careful not to make it too wet.

Add the fish sauce, fermented anchovies (if using) and sugar. Sprinkle with spring onion and coriander before serving.

MEAT

Meat is a popular part of the diet in Thailand, particularly pork. You've probably noticed by now that most of my recipes in the other chapters also contain pork-even including some salads. This is how Thais add protein to their diet, and it also enhances the flavour of the dishes. Beef is also popular, although slightly pricier. Lamb, however, is virtually unknown, which is why I haven't included any lamb dishes in this book. But please feel free to use it as a substitute in any of my recipes — it's fine to do so.

When I was young, we didn't have a supermarket nearby. My family always made trips to the market in town to get our weekly supplies. It might have been a bit weird considering my age, but I used to love these trips, as I got to pick the ingredients for my favourite dinner, which was garlic pork with sticky rice wrapped in a banana leaf parcel. My family has been getting its great quality meat from the family butcher you see in the picture here ever since I can remember, and they are still trading even today as I am writing this book. The beauty of this way of life is that you become friends with many of your local traders. I suppose it is the same way in many small villages across the UK, where everyone knows each other.

Nowadays, living in London, I often buy meat from the supermarket as it suits my busy life; I buy the best quality meat I can find, though, and when I can, I get it from my local butcher. I would encourage you to do the same. Look for good, fresh meat with a rich, vibrant, eye-catching colour and firm texture. You might be surprised to find that it doesn't cost that much more.

THAI BBQ PORK

Mu ping หมูปิ้ง

Carts selling barbecued pork are a common sight on Thai streets. Thais love to eat barbecued pork any time of the day: for breakfast, lunch, dinner, supper or as a snack. This incredibly simple and effective dish is great if you're having a barbecue with friends, or simply to enjoy as a family meal. In this recipe I use pork tenderloin, which is not too lean (the fat will help to keep it moist when cooking), together with a couple of teaspoons of brandy in the marinade. But you can use pretty much any other type of alcohol, as its purpose is to help break up the enzymes in the meat and tenderise it, so feel free to use red wine, white wine, rum or whisky. Some Thais also use pineapple juice, green papaya sap or baking soda, depending on what's available in their cupboard.

For best results, marinate the meat in the fridge overnight, or try putting the marinated pork on wooden barbecue skewers and freezing it for a few days before cooking – this'll give you amazingly tender meat to show off to your guests. But don't defrost the skewers in the microwave or you'll toughen the meat; leave it to defrost naturally in the fridge, or cook from frozen. And don't forget the steaming hot sticky rice!

Prep time
10 mins

Cooking time
15 mins

Marinate time
2 hours minimum

Serves
4

5–6 garlic cloves
8–10 coriander roots
¼ tsp freshly ground white pepper
800 g pork loin, cut into ½ cm slices
4 tbsp coconut milk (or substitute soya or fresh whole milk)
4 tbsp sunflower oil
3 tbsp light soy sauce
2–3 tbsp honey
1 tbsp fish sauce
1 tbsp oyster sauce
2 tsp brandy (optional)
2 tsp dark soy sauce
Pinch of salt
Barbecue skewers

Pound the garlic, coriander roots and pepper in a pestle and mortar until it forms a rough paste. Transfer to a bowl, and add the pork and all the remaining seasoning ingredients to it. Mix together well and leave to marinate in the fridge for at least 2 hours, or overnight for an even better result.

If using wooden skewers, soak them in water for about 15–20 minutes. Thread the marinated pork onto the skewers and then grill under a medium heat or on a barbecue for 15 minutes or until cooked.

For extra tenderness and a smoky flavour, continually brush the excess marinade onto the pork while it's cooking.

PORK IN GARLIC AND PEPPER

Mu thot kra thiam phrik thai หมูทอดกระเทียมพริกไทย

This amazing garlicky pork dish reminds me of my childhood. My mum and dad used to make it for me and my siblings, usually in the last few days before a trip to the market to restock, and it never failed to satisfy us fussy kids. Because the recipe for this gorgeous dish has a nice short list of ingredients, I was able to learn how to make it at a very young age. Nowadays, my husband and daughter often ask me to make it for them and never seem to get bored of it. All you need for this dish is a bit of meat and a few things you'd normally find in your 'Asian cupboard'.

Prep time
10 mins

Cooking time
10 mins

Serves
4–6

Top tip

Try to leave to marinate for 10-15 minutes. This will really make a difference!

---

800 g pork loin
6-8 garlic cloves, crushed
10 coriander roots or coriander stalks, finely chopped (optional)
Large pinch of freshly ground black or white pepper
3-4 tbsp light soy sauce
1 tbsp fish sauce
1 tsp dark soy sauce
Pinch of salt
100 ml oil of your choice, for frying

Bash the pork a few times with a meat tenderiser before slicing the meat; this will help it stay tender when cooked.

In a large bowl, mix together the pork, garlic, coriander roots, pepper, soy sauces, fish sauce and salt. You can then cook the dish straight away, but for the best results I recommend leaving it to marinate in the fridge for at least 10 minutes to half an hour.

Shallow fry the marinated meat in the oil over a medium heat for about 7-8 minutes or until the pork is golden brown.

STIR-FRIED PORK WITH HOLY BASIL

Phat ka phrao mu ผัดกะเพราหมู

The simplicity of this stir-fried dish makes it a classic Thai street food. You should be able to knock this together from scratch in ten or fifteen minutes. Pork is a big thing in Thailand, so I use it for this recipe, but you can also use beef, lamb, chicken or whatever your favourite meat is instead. If you cannot get Thai holy basil, you can substitute Mediterranean basil leaves, which are commonly available, but they tend to have a milder taste so I suggest doubling up on the amount. Most Thai street stalls add a heap of powdered MSG (monosodium glutamate) to enhance the flavour, but I see no benefit in using it, so I've replaced it with a pinch of sugar, which enhances and brings together the different tastes. Try topping this with a runny-yolked fried egg and eating it with hot steamed jasmine rice … Mmm!

Prep time
5 mins

Cooking time
10 mins

Serves
4

4–5 tbsp light-flavoured oil
1 medium onion, finely chopped
4–5 garlic cloves, crushed
500 g lean minced pork
3–5 bird's eye chillies, chopped
200 g holy basil leaves, washed and rinsed (or 400 g Mediterranean basil)
80 g green beans, rinsed and cut into 1 cm lengths
100 ml water
4–5 tbsp light soy sauce
2 tbsp fish sauce
1 tbsp dark soy sauce
Pinch of caster sugar

Heat the cooking oil in a wok or frying pan on a high heat for 30 seconds. Add the onion and garlic and stir—fry for 30 seconds

Add the pork and the chillies (if using) and cook, stirring, for 3 minutes or until the pork is cooked (the meat will change from pink to a whitish-brown colour).

Add the basil leaves and green beans, and cook for 1-2 minutes. Add the water, the light and dark soy sauce, the fish sauce and the sugar, stirring for another few minutes. Remove from the heat and serve straight away.

STIR-FRIED BEEF IN OYSTER SAUCE

Nua nam man hoi เนื้อน้ำมันหอย

This Chinese-influenced dish has been embedded within Thai cuisine for many generations. This is a classic example of how you can knock something together from what you have in your Asian cupboard in no time at all. The ingredients are simple and straightforward. Many people like to marinate the beef for half an hour before cooking, to tenderise it, but you can also cook it straight away if you're hungry. This dish is best served with hot steamed jasmine rice.

Prep time
15 mins

Marinate time
30 mins

Cooking time
10 mins

Serves
4

800 g beef, sliced
5 garlic cloves, crushed
4 tbsp soy sauce
2 tbsp cooking wine or red wine
2 tbsp cornflour
2 tsp light brown sugar or caster sugar
6–8 tbsp oil of your choice
400 g broccoli, chopped into pieces
100 ml water or beef stock
8 spring onions, finely sliced
2 red chillies, sliced lengthways
3 tbsp oyster sauce
Pinch of freshly ground black pepper

In a large bowl, mix the beef, garlic, soy sauce, cooking wine, cornflour and sugar. For best results, leave to marinate for at least 30 minutes.

In a wok or large frying pan, heat the oil until very hot (dip the tip of a wooden spoon or wooden chopstick into the oil; if the oil bubbles, it's ready for frying). Gently add the marinated beef. Stir-fry for 2–3 minutes until the beef starts to turn brown.

Add the broccoli, spring onion, chilli, oyster sauce and the water. Stir-fry all the ingredients for a few more minutes until the beef and broccoli are cooked. Transfer to a plate and serve straight away.

PANANG CURRY WITH BEEF

Keang pha neang nuea แกงพะแนงเนื้อ

Panang curry paste is often confused with red curry paste. This is understandable, as the ingredients are very similar, but panang curry paste includes cumin and coriander seeds as well. So if you don't have any panang paste ready to hand, simply use red curry paste and add half a teaspoon each of ground cumin seeds and ground coriander seeds. Some people also like to replace half the panang paste with some massaman curry paste to make the dish milder. Serve with hot steamed jasmine rice.

Prep time
10 mins

Cooking time
20 mins

Serves
4

Top tip

Try to roast the peanuts yourself by tossing unroasted peanuts in a dry pan over a low heat for a few minutes, and then let them cool before adding them to the curry. This will give your curry an extra rich and toasty flavour.

500 g beef, thinly sliced
400 ml (1 can) coconut milk
2 tbsp panang curry paste (p.155)
150 ml beef stock or water
100 g green beans, trimmed and cut into 2.5 cm pieces
4 tbsp unsalted roasted peanuts, finely chopped
2 long red chillies, sliced lengthways
8-10 kaffir lime leaves, finely shredded
Handful of Thai sweet basil leaves (optional)
4 tbsp fish sauce
1 tbsp palm sugar
Large pinch of salt

Heat 2-3 tablespoons of the coconut milk in a deep saucepan over a medium heat. Add the curry paste and fry it for a few minutes or until the coconut milk begins to separate out. Add the beef and stir continuously for 2 more minutes, until the meat is slightly cooked.

Add the rest of the coconut milk, the stock or water, the beans, peanuts, chilli, and most of the kaffir lime and sweet basil leaves (if using; save a few of both for garnishing). Stir well and simmer, uncovered, for 10 minutes.

Add the fish sauce, sugar and salt and cook, stirring, for 2-3 minutes. Garnish with the remaining kaffir lime and sweet basil leaves before serving.

POULTRY

People in Thailand have a strong relationship with poultry, as it is an agricultural country. Many families in the countryside keep poultry birds in their backyards. My family lived in a suburban area, and even there my dad managed to get us some guinea fowls and turkeys to keep in the garden. We treated them as our pets, so it took me a while to get used to having turkey at Christmas when I first moved to the UK!

Chicken takes less time to cook than duck, but they can be handled in the same way. Thais prefer to leave meat on the bone, as it gives much more flavour to the dish. Whenever you roast a chicken, throw the leftover carcass in a large, deep pot with a few garlic cloves and a chopped turnip or carrot and simmer with a lid on for a few hours over low heat. Or, if you have a slow cooker, simply put the whole carcass into it, add just enough water to cover it, and then cook on the low setting for six hours. (Check out my stock recipe on page 159 for details.) Leave the resulting stock to cool completely before transferring to an airtight container, or to ice cube trays if you want small individual quantities. I have found that the plastic bags designed to store milk are also brilliant for storing other liquids such as stock. This way, you can keep your very own homemade stock for all manner of home cooking uses.

GREEN CURRY WITH CHICKEN

Keang khiao wan kai แกงเขียวหวานไก่

I probably don't need to explain much about this dish as I'm sure you've probably had or at least heard of Thai green curry before. The real question is, have you ever made a *'really good'* Thai green curry? Whatever your answer is, here's how to make one! Thai people use Thai green aubergines for this curry, but you can substitute a medium purple aubergine instead. Again, replace the bamboo shoots with red bell peppers if you're unable to source them. Serve with hot steamed jasmine or sticky rice

Prep time
15 mins

Cooking time
20 mins

Serves
4

400 ml (1 can) coconut milk
2 tbsp green curry paste (p.154)
500 g chicken breast or boneless thigh fillets, sliced
250 ml chicken stock
250 g Thai aubergines or 1 medium aubergine, cut into 2.5 cm chunks
250 g tinned bamboo shoots (optional)
2 medium carrots, finely sliced
Handful of Thai sweet basil leaves
10-12 kaffir lime leaves, finely shredded
3-4 long red chillies, finely sliced lengthways
3 fingerroots, crushed with the flat of a large knife and finely cut lengthways
3-4 tbsp fish sauce
1 tbsp palm sugar

Heat 2-3 tbsp of the coconut milk in a large saucepan over a medium heat and then add the green curry paste. Stir together for 2-3 minutes or until the coconut milk has separated.

Add the chicken and stir for a few minutes until the meat starts to change colour. Add the rest of the ingredients, saving a few of the sweet basil leaves and red chillies for garnish, and then simmer the curry for 15 minutes.

Sprinkle the serving bowls with the red chillies and the remaining sweet basil leaves before serving.

CHICKEN WITH GINGER AND SPRING ONION

Kai phat khing ไก่ผัดขิง

Forget your local takeaway – this stir-fry is perfect for a weeknight meal. Like most stir-fries, its list of ingredients is short, so you can even finish the cooking in less time than it would take for the delivery man to bring your dinner–and it's much healthier, too, as you know exactly what's gone in there. Personally, I like to use sunflower oil as it's light and doesn't affect the flavour of the food. Choose any other oil, if you prefer, such as hemp oil, light olive oil or rapeseed oil.

Prep time
10 mins

Cooking time
10 mins

Serves
4

Top tip

Use fresh ginger if you can, as it really does add a comforting warmth to the dish.

4–5 tbsp cooking oil
1 medium onion, finely sliced
3 garlic cloves, crushed
800 g chicken breast (about 4 fillets), thinly sliced
2 red bell peppers, thinly sliced
2 small chunks of ginger, peeled and finely sliced
4–5 whole spring onions, chopped
100 ml water
4 tbsp light soy sauce
1 tbsp fish sauce
2 tsp dark soy sauce
1 tsp oyster sauce (optional)
Pinch of caster sugar
Pinch of ground black pepper

Heat the oil in a wok or frying pan on a high heat until very hot (dip the tip of a wooden spoon or wooden chopstick into the oil; if the oil bubbles, it's ready for frying). Add the onion and garlic and stir continuously, cooking until the onion is golden brown.

Add the chicken and stir-fry for a further 3–4 minutes, or until the chicken is well cooked. Add the red peppers (if you're using them), ginger and spring onion, and continue to stir-fry for a few more minutes, until the peppers have softened.

Add the water, and season with fish sauce, light and dark soy sauce, oyster sauce (if using) and sugar, and cook for another 1–2 minutes.

Sprinkle with ground black pepper and stir through before serving.

MASSAMAN CURRY WITH CHICKEN

Keang massaman kai แกงมัสมั่นไก่

I still remember my first taste of massaman. It was at a small curry house in my home town when I was a child. I didn't even know what it was called, and I had to point out the yummy-looking thing to the lady who was serving. I liked the look of it because it looked less fiery than the other dishes on display. I found it incredibly comforting - wonderfully rich and creamy with a unique, delicate flavour - and since that moment it's officially been my favourite curry. Many people think this curry is complicated to cook, but really it takes no more effort than making a plate of spaghetti bolognese. Simply follow the steps below, and enjoy the experience. Serve this with the rice of your choice.

Prep time
15 mins

Cooking time
30 mins

Serves
4

600 ml coconut milk

4 tbsp massaman curry paste (p.156)

1.2 kg bone-in chicken thighs or drumsticks

1 large onion, cut into thin wedges

250 ml chicken stock, or 2 chicken stock cubes dissolved in 250 ml water

6 medium potatoes, cut into 2.5 cm chunks

4 medium carrots, cut into 2.5 cm chunks

85 g unsalted roasted peanuts or cashew nuts, divided (optional)

2 cinnamon sticks (optional)

2 bay leaves

3-4 tbsp fish sauce

3 tbsp tamarind sauce

1 tbsp palm sugar

Pinch of salt

Heat 2-3 tablespoons of coconut milk in a large saucepan over high heat. Add the curry paste and fry for a minute (add a little more coconut milk if it seems too dry), then stir together for 2-3 minutes or until the coconut milk has separated.

Add the chicken and onion and fry for about 5 minutes or until they're well coated and the meat is sealed.

Stir in the rest of the coconut milk along with the chicken stock. Add the potatoes, carrots, most of the peanuts (if using), the cinnamon sticks, bay leaves, fish sauce, tamarind sauce, sugar and salt. Bring to the boil and cook for 5 minutes, then lower the heat and simmer for a further 15 minutes until the sauce has reduced a little.

Sprinkle each bowl with some of the remaining peanuts before serving.

CHICKEN DRUMSTICKS IN HONEY SAUCE

Kai op sot nam phueng ไก่อบซอสน้ำผึ้ง

You can count on this mouth-watering dish being delicious every time. All you need do is to pile everything onto a baking tray and let the oven do the job for you. Drumsticks cook in a fraction of the time it would take to roast a whole chicken, making them perfect for your weeknight and weekend meals. For parties, you can marinate the drumsticks overnight in the fridge for the most tender meat ever. Enjoy the meat and deliciously crispy skin with hot sticky rice or steamed jasmine rice.

Or how about a Thai-style roast dinner for a change? Simply replace the drumsticks with a medium-sized whole chicken and increase the cooking time to approximately 1 hour and 20 minutes, or according to the seller's instructions.

Prep time
5 mins

Marinate time
30 mins

Cooking time
10 mins

Serves
4

1.2 kg chicken drumsticks or bone-in thighs
2 stalks lemongrass, finely chopped
4-5 medium garlic cloves, crushed
Small handful of coriander roots or whole coriander, rinsed and roughly chopped
Large pinch freshly ground black pepper
3-4 tbsp light soy sauce
1 tbsp dark soy sauce
1 tbsp oyster sauce
1 tbsp clear honey

Pound the lemongrass (if using), garlic, coriander roots (if using) and black pepper in a pestle and mortar, or blend in a food processor until the mix forms a rough paste.

In a large oven-proof tray or dish, mix the paste with the light soy sauce, dark soy sauce, oyster sauce and honey. Taste and adjust the seasoning to taste, if required, before adding the chicken.

Mix the chicken with the sauce. If you don't have time you can cook them straight away, but for the best results, leave to marinate in the fridge for at least 30 minutes to 1 hour.

Preheat the oven to 200°C/Gas Mark 6. Place the drumsticks on a baking tray and put into the oven to roast for 25-30 minutes, turning after 15 minutes. Remove from the oven and serve.

ROASTED DUCK IN TAMARIND SAUCE

Pet ma kham เป็ดมะขาม

I was inspired to include this delicious duck dish because of its popularity among the people I have met in the UK. It's a dish that works very well whenever we have guests, so I thought I should share the recipe. This recipe is the quick version, as you can put the duck straight into the oven as soon as you've given it a good rub with salt and pepper. Cooking the duck at a high temperature will help to crisp the skin, and twenty minutes will give you a medium-rare finish. Leave it to cook for longer if you prefer your duck well done.

Prep time
10 mins

Cooking time
10 mins

Serves
4–6

Top tip

For a deeper, more infused flavour, try rubbing a piece of crushed star anise into the duck fillets with some salt and pepper, then leaving it to marinate in the fridge for at least two hours.

FOR THE DUCK

4 duck breast fillets
Pinch of Salt
Ground white pepper
4-5 tbsp cooking oil
2 shallots, finely sliced
Bunch of *kai lan*, or Chinese broccoli, chopped and steamed (you can substitute broccoli)
150 ml water
Handful of coriander, for garnish
4 tbsp roasted unsalted cashew nuts, for garnish

FOR THE SAUCE

250 ml tamarind sauce
2 tbsp palm sugar
2 tbsp tapioca flour
50 ml cold water
1 tbsp fish sauce
1 tbsp Thai white vinegar
2-4 dried chillies (optional)
Pinch of salt

Preheat the oven to 220°C/Gas Mark 7. Rub some salt and pepper onto the duck breasts. Place them on a baking tray or oven-proof dish, and cook them in the oven, skin side up, for 20-25 minutes. When they're ready, remove from the oven and loosely cover the dish with tin foil.

While the duck is cooking, heat the oil in a small frying pan, and then shallow fry the shallots until crispy. Take the pan off the heat to rest on the side once done.

Steam the *kai lan* in a small pan with 150 ml water for 7-8 minutes.

To make the sauce, heat the tamarind sauce and palm sugar in a saucepan over a medium heat for a few minutes. In a cup, mix the tapioca flour with the water, then pour into the saucepan. Gently stir for 1-2 minutes or until the sauce starts to thicken. Season with the fish sauce, vinegar, chillies and salt, then simmer for a few minutes until the sauce has reduced slightly.

Remove the duck breasts from the baking dish, and slice them up. Lay the steamed *kai lan* on a large serving plate, add the duck on top and pour the sauce over it. Sprinkle with the crispy shallots, fresh coriander and cashew nuts before serving.

ROASTED DUCK CURRY

Kaeng phet pet yang   แกงเผ็ดเป็ดย่าง

This delicious duck curry is a real treat. It contrasts the natural sweetness from the fruit with the saltiness of the fish sauce and the amazing fragrance of the herbs. When you first bake the duck it should be crispy on the outside but still rather raw on the inside, as it will be cooked again in the curry sauce. Serve this with hot steamed jasmine rice, or any rice of your choice.

Prep time
10 mins

Cooking time
25 mins

Serves
4

FOR THE DUCK
4 duck breast fillets
3 tbsp light soy sauce
1 tbsp dark soy sauce
1 tbsp honey

FOR THE CURRY
600 ml coconut milk
2 tbsp red curry paste (p.154)
200 ml chicken or vegetable stock
Handful of Thai sweet basil or basil leaves
8 kaffir lime leaves, finely chopped
10-12 slices of fresh or tinned pineapple, cut into bite-sized pieces
12-15 cherry tomatoes
12-15 green or red grapes
3-4 tbsp fish sauce
1 tbsp palm sugar
Pinch of sea salt

Preheat the oven to 220°C/Gas Mark 7. In a small bowl, mix the light soy sauce, dark soy sauce and honey, then rub onto the duck fillets. Place them in the oven for 15 minutes. Once cooked, remove from the oven and let the meat rest for 20 minutes. Cut the duck into slices approximately 1 cm thick.

To make the curry, heat 4-5 tbsp of coconut milk in a saucepan with the red curry paste on a medium heat. Stir well for 2-3 minutes or until the coconut milk has separated. Pour the rest of the coconut milk into the pan along with the stock, and stir for a few more minutes.

Turn up the heat and add the sliced duck, the sweet basil leaves (if using), kaffir lime leaves, pineapple, tomatoes and grapes. Add a little water if the curry seems too thick.

Season with 2-3 tbsp of the fish sauce, half the sugar and a pinch of salt. Leave to simmer for further 2-3 minutes. Taste and if necessary add more of the seasoning. Turn off the heat and serve.

FISH & SEAFOOD

In my home town, most of our fish and shellfish used to come from the local river or from farms. Being on the mainland, wild-caught seafood was a treat. The seafood van came to the market only on Friday afternoons, and my mum would be off on her moped before the whole town got there.

I love fish: it tastes great, is super-quick to cook, and luckily it happens to be healthy, too. If you have a fishmonger in your area, I would urge you to go and explore the options. A good fish should have bright and clear eyes, not cloudy and sunken ones. The gills should be bright red, and the skin should bounce back when gently pressed (you can ask your fishmonger to do this for you). Live shellfish should have shells that look moist and are tightly closed. Raw prawn meat should be firm, not soft. Most of the fish used in Thailand is white-fleshed, but you can also use pink-fleshed fish like salmon or trout in any of the recipes.

KING PRAWNS WITH ASPARAGUS

Kung phat no mai farang กุ้งผัดหน่อไม้ฝรั่ง

This beautiful prawn dish used to be a treat served at celebratory occasions in my family, because the asparagus had to be imported and the prawns were rather expensive where we lived, which was miles from the sea. I strongly encourage you to make the most of the readily available fresh ingredients in the UK, especially when asparagus is in season around springtime. This dish never fails to impress, and it only takes minutes to cook. Serve with hot steamed rice.

Prep time
10 mins

Cooking time
10 mins

Serves
4

Top tip

Because the sesame oil has a delicate flavour, I add it last, just before serving, to prevent its effect being lost.

4 tbsp oil of your choice

4 garlic cloves, crushed

400 g asparagus, cut into 2.5 cm long pieces

120 ml water

2 tbsp light soy sauce

1 tbsp oyster sauce

½ tsp caster sugar

700 g raw king prawns, cleaned and peeled

2 tbsp tapioca flour

2–3 tbsp cold water

¼ tsp freshly ground black pepper

1 tsp roasted sesame oil (optional)

Heat the cooking oil and the garlic in a wok or deep frying pan over a medium heat for 30 seconds to a minute. Add the asparagus, water, soy sauce, oyster sauce and sugar, and cook for 2–3 minutes before adding the prawns. Cook for a further 1–2 minutes, until the prawns start to change colour.

Mix the tapioca flour in a small cup or bowl with the cold water, stirring until it has dissolved. Add the tapioca mixture to the pan and stir continuously for a few minutes until the sauce thickens and turns clear.

Drizzle in the sesame oil and stir gently. Sprinkle with black pepper before serving.

KING PRAWNS WITH HERB-INFUSED GLASS NOODLES

Kung op wun sen กุ้งอบวุ้นเส้น

This is a delicious dish that is light but satisfying. The amazing aroma from the herbs will make your whole kitchen smell so festive. Traditionally it is cooked with a chunk of pork fat or with rendered pork fat. You might be feeling rather alarmed right now - but it really makes the dish incredibly flavourful and moist. If you want to steer clear of it, you can opt for pancetta or the oil of your choice.

Many restaurants serve this dish in a clay pot, but it can be a challenge to store the pot when not in use. Presumably, most of you will not have a clay pot at home, ready to hand, so for the sake of convenience use a casserole dish or deep baking dish instead, which is what I do. A seafood dipping sauce is the perfect accompaniment for this dish. (see page 157 for recipe). Serve as a main dish with hot steamed rice.

Prep time
10 mins

Cooking time
15 mins

Serves
4-6

200 g dried glass noodles, soaked in warm water for 20 minutes and cut into 10 cm long pieces
250 ml water
4 tbsp light soy sauce
2 tbsp oyster sauce
2 tbsp rendered pork fat or lard, or 4-5 tbsp vegetable oil
1 tsp sugar
8-10 coriander roots, chopped
4-5 garlic cloves, crushed
Medium-sized chunk of ginger, peeled and finely sliced
Pinch of ground star anise (optional)
400-500 g raw king prawns, cleaned and deveined
Handful of coriander leaves, for garnish

Preheat the oven to 220°C/Gas Mark 7. In a large bowl, mix together the noodles, water, soy sauce, oyster sauce, pork fat and sugar.

Into a clay pot or baking dish, put a layer of coriander root, garlic, ginger and star anise, then a layer of glass noodles. Finally, add the prawns on top.

Cover tightly with a lid or tin foil, place in the oven and cook for 10-12 minutes, then check to see that the prawns are cooking and the noodles are soft. If the noodles seem too dry, add a little water, stir through and cook for a further 2-3 minutes. Remove from the oven and garnish with the coriander leaves before serving.

STEAMED SEA BASS IN GARLIC AND LIME SAUCE

Pla nueng ma nao   ปลานึ่งมะนาว

This fantastic fish dish is hugely popular – and no wonder, since it's delicious, easy to put together and healthy. If you haven't got a steamer, you can also put the fish on a plate with three or four tablespoons of water, cover it with cling film and cook in a microwave on full power for three to five minutes, depending on the size of the fish. Thai people like their fish on the bone, but it can be more convenient to use fillets; but be cautious with the cooking time-make sure you don't overcook them. Enjoy with the steamed rice of your choice; this is great accompanied by sliced cucumbers too.

Prep time
5 mins

Cooking time
10 mins

Serves
4–6

Top tip

For the best results, use fresh fish and rub a little bit of salt all over it before cooking, then drain any liquid away before adding the sauce.

4 large sea bass fillets

Large pinch of salt

6 garlic cloves

2 red chillies, roughly chopped

4–5 tbsp lime juice

4 tbsp fish sauce

1 tsp caster or light brown sugar

Small handful of coriander leaves, for garnish

Clean the fish and pat dry, then rub with a little salt. Place the fish in a steamer and cook for 8–10 minutes.

While the fish is cooking, mix the garlic, chilli, lime juice, fish sauce and sugar together in a small bowl until the sugar has dissolved.

Transfer the fish to a serving platter and pour over the sauce. Sprinkle some coriander leaves on top before serving.

STEAMED MUSSELS WITH THAI HERBS

Hoi ma laeng phu op   หอยแมลงภู่อบ

Calling all seafood fanatics! This mussel dish is full of wonderful fragrances and is great either as a starter to get your appetite dancing, or as a big bowl as a main course to satisfy your hunger. They're best accompanied by my scrumptious spicy seafood dipping sauce (see page 157 for recipe) – a combination that's really worth trying. Or simply squeeze a wedge of lemon over them before serving.

Prep time
10 mins

Cooking time
10 mins

Serve
4

350 ml chicken or vegetable stock or water
2 large handfuls of Thai sweet basil, divided
4 stems lemongrass, cut into 2.5 cm pieces
4–5 bird's eye chillies, coarsely chopped
4–5 stalks green peppercorns (substitute 2 tsp whole black peppercorns)
1.6 kg mussels, cleaned and de-bearded (discard any open ones)
2–3 tbsp fish sauce
Pinch of brown sugar
2 lemons (optional)

In a wok or a deep saucepan, heat the chicken stock, most of the sweet basil, the lemongrass, chilli and the peppercorns until the liquid is bubbling.

Add the mussels and cover the pan with a lid. Cook for 5–8 minutes (stir halfway through to circulate the heat) until the mussels have all opened. Be careful not to overcook the mussels, as they'll become chewy. If necessary, remove the opened ones to the serving bowl and continue cooking the closed ones for another couple of minutes.

Season with the fish sauce and sugar. Before serving, discard any unopened mussels and add the remaining basil leaves. Serve straight away, squeezing lemon juice over the dish.

STEAMED SEA BREAM WITH GINGER AND SPRING ONIO

Pla nueng si io ปลานึ่งซีอิ๊ว

This zingy dish is perfect for those who are looking for something light, and the herbs give it an added health benefit. There is no chilli in this recipe (for once), which makes it an inviting and appetising dish for those who love experiencing new things. This is perfect served with hot steamed rice and stir-fried vegetables for a complete meal.

Prep time
5 mins

Cooking time
10 mins

Serves
4

Top tip

For the best results, use fresh fish and rub a little bit of salt all over it before cooking, then drain any liquid away before adding the sauce.

4 large sea bream fillets
Pinch of salt
Freshly ground white or black pepper
6 whole spring onions, roots removed and cut into 2.5 cm pieces
2 small pieces of ginger, peeled and finely sliced
3-4 tbsp water
2 tbsp light soy sauce
½ tsp caster sugar
Coriander leaves, for garnish

Rub the fish fillets with a little salt and pepper, and then cook in a steamer for 5 minutes.

Meanwhile, make the sauce by combining the spring onions, ginger, water, soy sauce and sugar in a small bowl.

After 5 minutes, once the fish is partly cooked, drain off any juices produced during the steaming. Pour the sauce mixture over the fish and cook for another 5-7 minutes or until cooked through. Garnish with the coriander leaves before serving.

DRY RED CURRY WITH SALMON

Chu chi pla salmon ฉู่ฉี่ปลาซาลม่อน

This particular type of curry is commonly made with fish, but you can also use other seafood, such as prawns, mussels or scallops – although the cooking time will vary. The fingerroots will bring out the aroma and flavour of the curry more, but if you can't find them, you can always compensate by adding a few more kaffir lime leaves: this way, you'll still achieve a fantastically rich and creamy curry in minutes.

Prep time
10 mins

Cooking time
10 mins

Serve
4

100 ml sunflower oil, for shallow frying
4 salmon fillets, rinsed and patted dry
400 ml (1 can) coconut milk
1 tbsp red curry paste (p.154)
6 kaffir lime leaves, finely shredded, divided
2 fingerroots, grated (optional)
1 fresh long chilli, deseeded and finely sliced (optional)
2 tbsp fish sauce
1 tbsp palm sugar or light brown sugar
120 ml chicken or vegetable stock, or water

Heat the oil in a heavy-based wok or frying pan until nearly smoking. Turn down the heat to medium and add the salmon, skin side down. Turn after 3 minutes and cook for another 2 minutes. Remove to a serving dish and set aside.

In a clean wok or large frying pan, heat 4–6 tbsp of coconut milk and the curry paste over a medium heat. Stir until the paste is smooth and the fat from the coconut milk separates.

Add the remaining coconut milk, the lime leaves (reserve a small amount for garnishing), fingerroot, chilli, fish sauce and palm sugar. Add the chicken stock (or water), stir well and simmer for about 5 more minutes until the sauce has reduced a little and the cream has separated, and then pour the sauce over the fish.

Garnish with the remaining lime leaves before serving.

STIR-FRIED MIXED SEAFOOD WITH CURRY POWDER

Ta le phat phong ka ri ทะเลผัดผงกะหรี่

The curry powder makes this dish really warm and earthy. This dish is surprisingly not very well-known in the West, but it is one of Thailand's most loved Chinese-Thai dishes. This is really satisfying with just a little bowl of hot jasmine rice.

Prep time
10 mins

Cooking time
10 mins

Serves
4

4–5 tbsp cooking oil of your choice
1 medium onion, peeled and finely sliced
4 garlic cloves, peeled and crushed
2 free-range eggs
200 ml chicken stock or whole milk or water
2 small pieces of ginger, peeled and finely sliced
2–3 tbsp light soy sauce
2 tbsp curry powder
1 tbsp chilli paste (optional)
1 tbsp fish sauce
1 tsp caster sugar
700 g mixed seafood, such as prawns, squid and mussels
4 spring onions, roughly chopped

Heat the oil in a wok or frying pan over high heat, then add the onion and garlic and fry until softened.

Push the garlic and onion to one side of the wok, then break the eggs into the other side of the pan and scramble lightly.

Add the chicken stock, ginger, soy sauce and curry powder, as well as the chilli paste (if using), the fish sauce and sugar. Cook, stirring, for a few minutes.

Add the seafood and stir-fry for a few more minutes until just cooked. Mix in the spring onion and check the seasoning, adjusting if necessary, before serving.

STIR-FRIED CLAMS WITH CHILLI PASTE AND BASIL

Hoi lai phat phrik phao หอยลายผัดพริกเผา

This is another dish well-loved in Thailand but little known in the West, which is why I feel it deserves a place in this book. The chilli paste plays a big part in the seasoning here; you can buy a jar from an Asian supermarket or online. Clean the clams by soaking them in cold water with a tablespoon of salt for fifteen or twenty minutes. After that, scoop the clams out of the water and scrub the shells with a sponge or brush to remove any grit, and rinse well.

The beautiful fragrance from the herbs, the strong taste of the chilli paste and the natural juices released by the clams give this dish so much flavour, you should hardly need to season the dish at all. Add the fish sauce sparingly to begin with, as you might not need as much as indicated here. If it tastes too salty, add a little water to dilute the flavour. Serve this with hot steamed rice.

Prep time
25 mins

Cooking time
10 mins

Serves
4

4–5 tbsp light-flavoured oil

1 medium onion, finely chopped

4 garlic cloves, crushed

1 kg clams in their shells, cleaned

Large handful of Thai sweet basil leaves

4–5 fingerroots, sliced lengthways

4–5 stalks green peppercorns

3–4 fresh chillies, coarsely chopped

2 tbsp fish sauce

1 tbsp roasted chilli paste

1 tsp caster sugar

4 tbsp water

Heat the oil in a wok or large frying pan, add in the onion and garlic, and stir-fry until soft and slightly browned.

Add the clams and stir-fry for a further 2–3 minutes, until the shells have opened slightly.

Throw in the basil leaves, finger-roots, green peppercorns and the remaining seasoning ingredients – adding a little less fish sauce to start with – and cook for a few more minutes. Add a little water if the mixture is too dry.

Check the flavour and adjust the seasoning to taste, and then serve straight away.

VEGETARIAN

We all know that there are so many good reasons to eat a diet full of fruits and vegetables. Whether you are a lifelong vegetarian or are choosing to eat more meat-free dishes, these recipes will make you love vegetables even more.

The whole idea of this book is to show you how to cook authentic Thai food using your everyday ingredients. As long as you have the basic Asian sauces in your cupboard, you'll be able to create a wide variety of delicious Thai vegetarian dishes really easily in your our home.

AUBERGINES WITH THAI SWEET BASIL

Ma kuea phat bai ho ra pha เมือดผัดใบโหระพา

This dish is another of my favourite stir-fries; it's great as a vegetarian and vegan main dish, or as a side dish for anyone. Best of all, it takes just minutes to put together. The freshness of the sweet basil leaves goes so well with the aubergines. Regular Mediterranean basil leaves make a good substitute for the Thai ones, although they're not as fragrant, so make sure you add an extra handful to compensate.

Prep time
5 mins

Cooking time
10 mins

Serves
4

4 tbsp sunflower oil, or other light-flavoured oil

1 medium onion, chopped

4 garlic cloves, crushed

2 large aubergines or 6 long Thai aubergines, chopped into bite-size pieces

2 fresh long chillies (include the seeds if you like it spicy)

100 ml water

120 g Thai basil leaves, divided

2–3 tbsp light soy sauce

½ tbsp yellow bean paste (substitute salted roasted peanuts)

Pinch of sugar

Lime juice (optional)

Heat the oil in a wok or large frying pan over a medium heat. Add the onion and garlic, and stir-fry until soft and lightly browned. Add the aubergine and chillies and stir-fry for about 5 minutes. When the pan gets dry, add enough of the water to keep the ingredients frying nicely until the aubergine is soft and its white flesh is almost translucent.

When the aubergine is cooked, add the sweet basil leaves (leaving a few for garnishing). Add the soy sauce, the yellow bean paste and sugar, and stir-fry for a couple more minutes.

Check the seasoning. If it's not salty enough, add a little more fish sauce. If it's too salty, add 1 tbsp lime juice or a little more water.

MIXED VEGETABLES IN OYSTER SAUCE

Phat phak nam man hoi ผัดผักน้ำมันหอย

This classic recipe is most commonly served as a side dish along with a main course. It's incredibly easy to make, so it's perfect for all occasions, especially weeknights. The selection of vegetables I've suggested here is just to give you an idea – you can also use any other vegetables you have on hand. Most supermarkets have packets of mixed vegetables on their shelves, and frozen vegetables work just as well – simply cook for a few minutes longer. The general rule is to add the hard vegetables first, and softer ones later.

Prep time
5 mins

Cooking time
5–7 mins

Serves
4

4 tbsp light-flavoured oil
½ head broccoli, chopped into florets
2 medium carrots, unpeeled and sliced into ½ cm rounds
2 green bell peppers, sliced
10 mange tout, ends trimmed off
10 chestnut mushrooms, halved
4–6 tbsp water
2 tbsp light soy sauce
2 tbsp oyster sauce
2 tsp dark soy sauce
Pinch of sugar

Heat the oil in a wok or large frying pan over a high heat until hot (dip the tip of a wooden spoon or wooden chopstick into the oil; if it bubbles, it's ready for frying).

Add the broccoli, carrot, green pepper and mange tout, and stir-fry for about 3 minutes. Leave the mushrooms until later, as they need less cooking. Add a few tablespoons of water to the pan.

Once the vegetables start to soften, add the mushrooms and continue to stir-fry for a few more minutes.

Add both soy sauces and the oyster sauce, sugar and a few more tablespoons of water. Cook while stirring for 1 more minute, before transferring to a plate to serve.

THAI OMELETTE WITH GARLIC AND MUSHROOMS

Kai jiao het sap   ไข่เจียวเห็ดสับ

Because of this recipe's simplicity, it hardly ever makes it into Thai cookbooks. I hope that this recipe will at least give you an idea of what you can achieve in next to no time. The secret to a gorgeously crispy Thai omelette is to use sizzling hot oil and a few drops of lime juice. Run the mixture through a sieve to help add air to the beaten egg just before it hits the pan.

   If you don't have a really large pan or wok, you can divide the mixture to make two or four omelettes rather than a single big one. With a little bit of practice in this method, this dish will soon become your favourite five-minute meal. For a wonderfully vivid colour, try adding a pinch of ground turmeric to the egg mix. Serve with hot steamed jasmine rice, sliced fresh cucumber and Sriracha sauce, or with any of the relishes. (See recipes on page 68-71).

Prep time
5 mins

Cooking time
5 mins

Serves
4 as a light meal

4-5 tbsp light-flavoured oil
150 g white or chestnut mushrooms, finely chopped
1 clove garlic, crushed
8 medium free-range eggs
1 tsp cornflour (optional)
1 tbsp light soy sauce
2 tsp oyster sauce
½ tsp ground turmeric (Optional)
Dash of lime juice

Heat 1 tablespoon of the oil in a wok or a large frying pan, and stir in the mushroom and garlic. Fry for about 1 minute, then transfer to a plate and leave on the side to rest.

   Heat the remaining oil in the same pan on a high heat until just smoking. While the wok is heating up, crack the eggs into a bowl with some cornflour (if using) and beat vigorously with a fork to let air in. Season with the light soy sauce, oyster sauce and turmeric, if you're using it. Add a few drops of lime juice to the mix (this will help to add fluffiness).

   When the wok is ready, return the garlic and mushrooms to it. Pour the egg mixture through a sieve into the wok. Let the egg spread out in the pan and form into a pancake, cooking for 2 minutes or so. When it turns golden brown – after 2-3 minutes – turn it over and cook the other side for a few more minutes. Remove to a plate and serve.

SOUTHERN-STYLE YELLOW CURRY WITH PINEAPPLE

Kaeng sup pa rot แกงสับปะรด

This traditional southern curry is supposed to be quite hot. I've toned this recipe down to make it more accessible to those who are less familiar with Thai cooking. But feel free to add more paste to the recipe if you can handle it. Making the paste is nice and easy (see page 156 for recipe). If you eat shellfish, you might like to add some mussels or king prawns. This is delicious with hot steamed rice.

Prep time
15 mins

Cooking time
30 mins

Serves
4

400 ml (1 can) coconut milk
2 tbsp yellow curry paste (p.156)
600 g fresh or tinned pineapple, coarsely chopped
400 ml vegetable stock
200 g green beans, cut into 5 cm lengths
4 tbsp fish sauce (substitute soy sauce to make vegan)
2 tbsp tamarind sauce
2 tsp palm sugar
Large pinch of salt

Fry 2 tablespoons of the curry paste in a medium-sized saucepan with 4-5 tablespoons of coconut milk, until the milk has separated.

Add the rest of the coconut milk, the pineapple, vegetable stock and green beans, then cover the pan and cook for 10 minutes over medium heat.

Season with the fish or soy sauce, tamarind sauce, palm sugar and salt. Stir well, then cover and simmer for 10 more minutes.

GREEN BEANS IN RED CURRY PASTE

Thua fak yao phat phrik kaeng ถั่วฝักยาวผัดพริกแกง

This recipe takes minutes to cook but can please a hungry crew, making it perfect for a weeknight meal. Traditionally, most people add pork to this dish, but I have replaced this with cashew nuts as an alternative protein. Try serving it topped with a fried egg for each person and a bowl of hot steamed jasmine rice for a complete meal.

Prep time
5 mins

Cooking time
10 mins

Serves
4

Top tip

You can also replace the cashew nuts with peanuts or any firm tofu for variety.

---

4 tbsp sunflower oil or other light-flavoured oil

1 medium onion, sliced

4 garlic cloves, crushed

2 tbsp red curry paste (p.154)

800 g green beans, chopped into 2.5 cm pieces

250 g unsalted cashew nuts or firm tofu

10-12 kaffir lime leaves, cut in half

100 ml vegetable stock or water

2 tbsp light soy sauce

1 tsp caster sugar

Heat the oil in a wok or large frying pan over a medium heat. When the oil is hot, add the onion and garlic and fry, stirring, until the onion has softened.

Add the curry paste and the beans, cashew nuts and lime leaves. Add the vegetable stock or water, and cook, stirring, for 2-3 minutes.

Season with the soy sauce and sugar, and cook for 3 minutes or so before serving.

PUMPKIN AND SUGAR SNAP CURRY

Kaeng phet fak thong แกงเผ็ดฟักทอง

Both pumpkin and sugar snap peas are rich in vitamins and minerals. Butternut squash makes a good substitute if you can't find a nice ripe pumpkin, but its flavour may not be as intense. Sugar snap peas cook very quickly, so add them towards the end to preserve their goodness. For extra protein, add some hard tofu to the dish — but do so ten minutes after the pumpkin goes in, as it doesn't take as long to cook.

Prep time
10 mins

Cooking time
25 mins

Serves
4

400 ml (1 can) coconut milk
2 tbsp red or green curry paste (p.154)
600 g pumpkin, peeled and chopped into 2.5 cm cubes and then soaked in cold salted water for 10 mins
250 ml vegetable stock
150 g sugar snap peas, washed and trimmed
2 tbsp light soy sauce (or 2 tsp sea salt)
2 tsp palm sugar
120 g Thai sweet basil leaves

Heat 2 tablespoons of the coconut milk along with the curry paste in a deep saucepan over high heat, and stir well until the milk starts to separate.

Add the pumpkin, stir through and cook for a few minutes.

Add the rest of the coconut milk and the vegetable stock, and bring the pot to a boil; then reduce the heat to medium, cover the pan with a lid and leave to cook for 20 minutes, or until the pumpkin is cooked through.

Add the sugar snaps, and season with the light soy sauce and sugar. Stir through the sweet basil leaves shortly before serving.

DUCK EGGS WITH SHALLOTS AND TAMARIND SAUCE

Khai lok khoei ไข่ลูกเขย

This popular dish has a funny name in Thai which translated means 'son-in-law's eggs'. According to one tale, before the marriage of a young man and his bride, the bride's father and the groom-to-be had a cooking challenge. Knowing how much the bride loved omelettes, they both planned to cook her one, with the finest duck eggs they could find. But the night before the contest, the bride's father boiled the groom's eggs. The next day, during the contest, the groom cracked open his eggs, only to find them hard-boiled. Instead of giving up, he decided to take a chance and deep-fry the eggs, devising a delicious sauce to go with them. The dish has been named after him ever since, so you can probably guess who won the challenge! Serve this as a main dish with hot steamed rice and sliced fresh cucumber and lettuce.

Prep time
10 mins

Cooking time
25 mins

Serves
4

8 free-range duck eggs
150 ml oil, for deep frying
4 medium shallots, finely sliced and deep-fried for 2 minutes
Handful of coriander leaves
2–4 whole dried chillies

FOR THE SAUCE
2 tbsp light-flavoured oil
6 tbsp fish sauce
4 tbsp tamarind sauce
4 tbsp palm sugar
2 shallots, sliced
4 tbsp water

PREPARING THE EGGS: Boil the duck eggs for 7 minutes, then cool them under running water before peeling them.

In a deep non-stick pan, heat the oil on a medium heat until it is very hot (dip the end of a wooden spoon or wooden chopstick into the oil; if it bubbles, it's ready for frying), and then carefully add the boiled eggs whole. Shallow fry the eggs for 5–10 minutes until they turn golden brown. Turn the eggs in the oil gently to prevent them from burning. Remove the eggs from the oil using a slotted spoon or small strainer, transfer to a plate and leave to cool down.

PREPARING THE SAUCE: Heat the oil in a small frying pan over low heat. Add the fish sauce, tamarind sauce, sugar and shallots. Stir continuously for about 5 minutes, until the sauce reduces and thickens.

TO SERVE: Gently cut the eggs into halves or quarters and place on a serving plate. Pour the sauce over the eggs. Garnish with the coriander, chillies and deep-fried shallots.

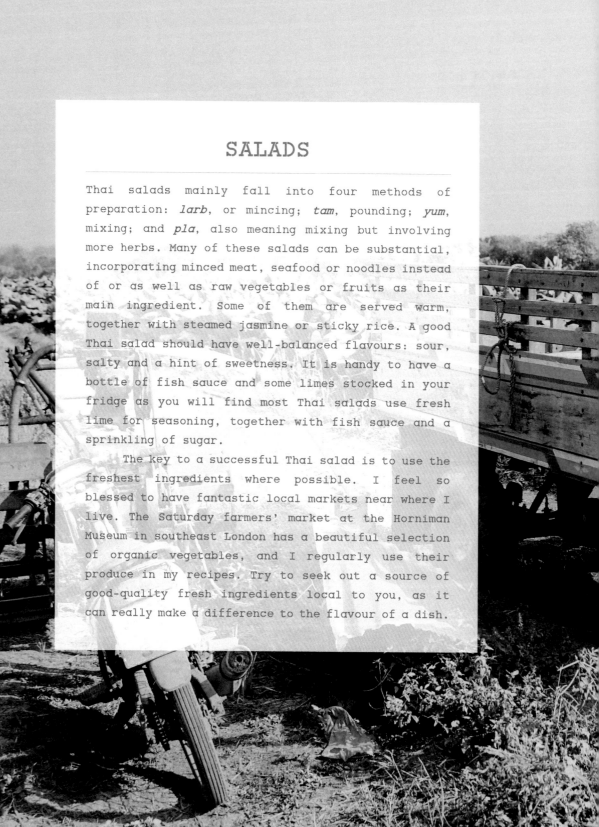

SALADS

Thai salads mainly fall into four methods of preparation: *larb*, or mincing; *tam*, pounding; *yum*, mixing; and *pla*, also meaning mixing but involving more herbs. Many of these salads can be substantial, incorporating minced meat, seafood or noodles instead of or as well as raw vegetables or fruits as their main ingredient. Some of them are served warm, together with steamed jasmine or sticky rice. A good Thai salad should have well-balanced flavours: sour, salty and a hint of sweetness. It is handy to have a bottle of fish sauce and some limes stocked in your fridge as you will find most Thai salads use fresh lime for seasoning, together with fish sauce and a sprinkling of sugar.

The key to a successful Thai salad is to use the freshest ingredients where possible. I feel so blessed to have fantastic local markets near where I live. The Saturday farmers' market at the Horniman Museum in southeast London has a beautiful selection of organic vegetables, and I regularly use their produce in my recipes. Try to seek out a source of good-quality fresh ingredients local to you, as it can really make a difference to the flavour of a dish.

SPICY GREEN PAPAYA SALAD

Som Tam Thai สัมตำไทย

This wonderful crunchy and tangy salad is arguably the nation's favourite. There's quite a bit of regional variation in recipes for it, depending on the local accessibility of ingredients. The version I use is a classic in central Thailand and Bangkok. Traditionally, the salad is crushed in a pestle and mortar to bring out the juice from the fresh ingredients, but don't worry if you don't have one – simply put the salad in a heavy mixing bowl and pound gently with the end of a rolling pin instead. Some of my non-Thai friends are not really convinced by the rather peculiar smell of the dried shrimp in this recipe; if you feel the same, cooked fresh prawns are a perfect substitute. Green papaya is rare and pricey in the West, so I usually replace it with a couple of carrots or some kohlrabi or raw swede instead, which means I can make this as often as I like.

This recipe would be enough to serve as a side dish for 4 people. I would strongly recommend making this twice from scratch rather than doubling up the amount if having more guests – it doesn't taste as good when made in a big batch for some reason. This refreshing salad goes incredibly well with Chicken Drumsticks in Honey Sauce (see page 92 for recipe) and hot sticky rice. Get crushing!

Prep time
15 mins

Cooking time
10 mins

Serves
4 as a side dish

3 large garlic cloves

2 whole bird's eye chillies

8-10 green beans, trimmed and cut into 2.5 cm long pieces

8-10 cherry tomatoes, halved

200 g green papaya, roughly grated

½ medium carrot, roughly grated

6 tbsp lime juice

5-6 tbsp fish sauce

1 tbsp grated palm sugar, brown sugar or honey

½ tbsp tamarind sauce (optional)

2 tbsp dried baby shrimps (*kung haeng*), well-rinsed and patted dry, or cooked king prawns

2 tbsp whole unsalted roasted peanuts

In a pestle and mortar, roughly crush the garlic and chilli. Add the raw beans and tomatoes and pound a few times, just to bruise them and extract their juices. Add the papaya and carrot. Keep pounding lightly.

Add the lime juice, fish sauce, sugar and the tamarind juice if you're using it. Make sure the sugar dissolves properly, leaving no lumps.

Mix together and transfer to a serving dish, and sprinkle on the shrimps and peanuts.

GLASS NOODLE AND KING PRAWN SALAD

Yam wun sen kung ยำวุ้นเส้นกุ้ง

This light and incredibly refreshing dish is packed with flavour, and is another Thai favourite that you can expect to find on the menu no matter where you go: at restaurants, parties or on the family dinner table. The glass noodles are delicate, so you don't want to overcook them, otherwise the dish will become mushy. You might like to cut the noodles into four to make them easier to eat, as they are very long. After you cook them, try to shake off as much excess water as possible, as any remaining water will dilute the sharp, fresh flavour of the overall dish. I use a small 50 gram pack, which makes a perfect portion for one hungry person or a fantastic side dish to share.

   Again, I would recommend making this dish twice from scratch rather than doubling up the amount to serve more people – it doesn't taste as good when made in a big batch. The dish should taste tangy – sour from the lime and salty from the fish sauce, with the sugar marrying the flavours together. Enjoy at its best: immediately!

Prep time
10 mins

Cooking time
10 mins

Serves
4

250 g raw king prawns
100 g minced pork
50 g glass noodles
20 g Chinese celery leaves, cut into 2 cm pieces
2 shallots, finely sliced (or ½ medium-sized onion)
2 bird's eye chillies (deseeded if preferred), coarsely chopped
3 tbsp fish sauce
3 tbsp lime juice
1 tbsp caster light brown sugar
50 g cherry tomatoes, halved
Handful of coriander leaves, for garnish

Bring a medium-sized pot of water to the boil, add the prawns and minced pork, and blanch them for 3 minutes. Drain well. In a fresh pan of boiling water, blanch the noodles for 2-3 minutes or until al dente, then drain. Run the noodles under cold water immediately to stop them continuing to cook in the residual heat, and then leave to drain.

   Mix the Chinese celery, shallots, chilli, fish sauce, lime juice and sugar in a bowl. (I use shallots in this recipe as they give a sweeter flavour than an onion, but a little onion is an acceptable substitute.) If you wish, you can let the shallots and chillies soak in the dressing for a few minutes, as this it will tone down the heat.

   For a good, intense flavour, first mix the dry ingredients in a bowl: the cooked minced pork, prawns, glass noodles and tomatoes. Then pour the dressing over them. Toss the whole dish gently and garnish with coriander leaves.

PORK SALAD WITH GARLIC, LIME AND FRESH MINT

Mu ma nao หมูมะนาว

This tangy salad takes minutes to make. The key is not to overcook the meat, or it will become chewy. Try to slice the pork as thinly as possible to keep it tender. The refreshing aroma of mint leaves is designed to counteract the pungency of the garlic, so you can enjoy as much of the dish as you like! A small bowl of cucumber sticks on the side makes a perfect companion to this dish; serve with rice to make a complete meal.

Prep time
5 mins

Cooking time
5 mins

Serves
4

½ head broccoli, chopped into small florets
700 g pork shoulder, finely sliced
8-10 garlic cloves, finely sliced
2 fresh bird's eye chillies (deseeded if preferred), coarsely chopped
4-5 tbsp lime juice
4-5 tbsp fish sauce
2 tsp caster or light brown sugar
Large handful of fresh mint leaves

In a medium-sized saucepan, bring some water to the boil. Blanch the broccoli for 2-3 minutes and then add the pork.

Boil for a further 2-3 minutes or until the meat is cooked through. Drain well and transfer to a serving plate.

To make the dressing, add all the other ingredients to a bowl and stir well, until the sugar has dissolved. Pour over the pork and broccoli, and serve.

SPICY MINCED CHICKEN WITH TOASTED GROUND RICE

Larb kai ลาบไก่

This salad is originally from northeastern Thailand but has become one of the most popular salads in the country. The infused aroma of toasted ground rice and mint leaves makes it tangy and delicious. Traditionally it's served warm, with hot sticky rice and a wedge of fresh cabbage and cucumber to counteract the heat. The word *larb* in Thai means mincing of meat. I've used chicken here, but you can also use minced pork or beef, duck meat or even squid with this recipe. This dish should taste tangy, so taste and add more lime juice at the end if needed. You can also save time for future recipes by batch-cooking the tossed ground rice and keeping it in an airtight container in the cupboard (see page 158 for recipe). This recipe is so good, I have no doubt you'll find yourself making it over and over again.

Prep time
25 mins

Cooking time
10 mins

Serves
4

2 tbsp uncooked glutinous rice or long-grain rice

750 g chicken breast or 4 fillets

1 medium carrot, finely grated

4 shallots, finely sliced

Large handful of mint leaves, rinsed

Large handful of coriander leaves and stalks, rinsed and roughly chopped

10-12 blades fresh sawtooth coriander (culantro), or 10 spring onions, roots removed and coarsely chopped

1 small stem galangal, finely chopped or (optional) 12 kaffir lime leaves, finely sliced

6-8 tbsp freshly squeezed lime juice (about 2 ½ medium limes)

4 tbsp chicken stock or water

5 tbsp fish sauce

6-8 tbsp freshly squeezed lime juice (about 2 ½ medium limes)

1-2 tsp dried chilli flakes

Toss the rice grains in a small frying pan on a low heat. Stir constantly until the rice turns golden brown (this should take about 2-3 minutes). Remove from the heat and leave to cool, then grind in a pestle and mortar, or blend in a food processor for 30 seconds.

Chop the chicken breast into small pieces and then blend in a food processor to a rough texture. Bring a pan of water to the boil, and poach the minced chicken for 2-3 minutes or until the chicken is thoroughly cooked (the meat will turn whitish). Drain through a colander, shaking off any excess water still clinging to the chicken.

Put all the ingredients, including the ground rice and the minced chicken, in a bowl and mix well. Adjust the seasoning to taste, and serve.

SPICY PRAWNS WITH THAI HERBS

Pla kung   พล่ากุ้ง

This light and elegant salad has all four main elements of Thai flavour: sour, salty, hot and sweet. The kaffir lime leaves will add a great aroma to the salad, but you can leave them out if you can't get hold of any. Many Thai cooks like to add a small amount of roasted chilli paste to the dressing, but again it is not essential.

Like most Thai salads, this dish should be led by the sourness, followed by the salty and hot flavours. It is so uplifting and refreshing; combined with classic Thai herbs, this dish will make your taste buds explode with delight. This is great served with steamed rice.

Prep time
20 mins

Cooking time
10 mins

Serves
4

Top tip

The trick is to cook the prawns to medium-rare – about 1 to 2 minutes is all you need, and this will preserve the prawns' natural sweetness and prevent them from becoming chewy.

750 g medium-sized king prawns, cleaned, shelled and deveined
4 stalks lemongrass, finely sliced
4 kaffir lime leaves, finely sliced
2–3 shallots, finely sliced
3–4 bird's eye chillies (deseeded if preferred), coarsely chopped
5 tbsp freshly squeezed lime juice (juice of about 2 limes)
5 tbsp fish sauce
1 tbsp roasted chilli paste (*nam phrik phao*; optional)
1 tsp palm sugar
Large handful of fresh mint leaves

In a small bowl, prepare the dressing by mixing the lemongrass, kaffir lime leaves (if using), shallot, chilli, lime juice, fish sauce, roasted chilli paste (if using) and sugar. Mix well until the sugar has dissolved and then set aside.

In a medium-sized saucepan, heat about 500 millilitres of water and bring to a boil.

Turn the heat down to medium and then add the prawns. Cook them until they turn opaque, then remove from the heat and drain well.

Transfer the prawns to a serving bowl, add the dressing and toss lightly. Taste the salad and adjust the seasoning if necessary.

Sprinkle the salad with mint leaves and serve immediately.

CHARGRILLED AUBERGINE & TOASTED COCONUT FLAKES

Yam ma kuea phao ยำมะเขือเผา

Surprisingly, this salad is not as well-known as it deserves to be. It's normally made with long Thai aubergines, which are long and green, but if you can't find them, the big purple aubergines work just fine. By now you've probably noticed that Thais add pork or other meat to most of their salads, mainly to add protein to the dish and to make it more substantial. For a vegetarian version, simply replace the meat with a meat substitute such as minced Quorn, or add more boiled eggs. Light soy sauce makes a good substitute for the fish sauce here, too. Serve as part of a main meal with hot steamed rice of your choice.

Prep time
5 mins

Cooking time
15–30 mins

Serves
4

4 long Thai aubergines, or 2 medium purple aubergines
4 tbsp light-flavoured oil
75 g lean minced pork (or beef)
4 tbsp desiccated coconut
2 shallots, finely chopped
4 spring onions, roots removed and chopped into 1 cm pieces
2 bird's eye chillies (deseeded if preferred), coarsely chopped
4 tbsp fish sauce
4 tbsp lime juice
2 tbsp semi-skimmed milk
2 tsp caster or light brown sugar
1 tsp chilli paste (optional)
Small handful of coriander leaves, for garnish
1 medium-sized free-range egg, hard-boiled, peeled and halved.

Cut the aubergines into slices lengthways, so that you end up with long, flat pieces about 1 cm thick. Drizzle the oil over the cut aubergine, place on a baking tray and grill under a medium heat for 8–10 minutes, turning halfway through. (You can also cook the aubergine in the oven for 20 minutes on 220°C/Gas Mark 7.)

While the aubergines are cooking, boil the egg with shell in a small saucepan on high heat for 10 minutes. Once done, remove the shells and cut in half. Set aside.

In a small saucepan, bring a pot of water to the boil and poach the pork for 1–2 minutes or until cooked (the flesh will change colour from pink to white-brown). Be careful not to overcook the pork as this will remove too much of its flavour. Drain and shake as much excess water from the pork as possible.

In a dry wok or frying pan, toss the coconut flakes on a low heat for a few minutes, stirring constantly until they turn golden brown.

Mix the dry ingredients-the aubergine, pork and coconut-together in a bowl, and then add the remaining ingredients. Transfer to a serving dish or bowl, and garnish with the coriander leaves.

CRISPY TUNA WITH GREEN MANGO DRESSING

Yam pla tuna fu   ยำปลาทูน่าฟู

This wonderful salad is traditionally made with grilled catfish, but tinned tuna is a great substitute, especially since it's much more readily available than catfish. Use tuna that's tinned in oil rather than brine, as this will give you a nice crispy finish. Sea bream is also a good fish to use for this dish because of its firm texture; if you're using fresh sea bream, first grill the fillets for five minutes and then pat them dry thoroughly before frying.

For this recipe, you want to make sure the fish is nice and fluffy, so the oil you use for the deep-frying needs to be quite hot – about 170–180°C. If you can't find a green mango, a fresh tangy cooking apple makes a great substitute. I use rice bran oil for this recipe as it has a high smoke point and a mild flavour, but any other cooking oil will do – though the lighter its colour, the better.

Prep time
10 mins

Cooking time
20 mins

Serves
4

FOR THE TUNA
500 g tinned tuna in oil
(approx. 2 cans), drained
250 g breadcrumbs or panko
400 ml plus 1 tbsp rice
bran oil

FOR THE MANGO DRESSING
6 tbsp fish sauce
2 tsp caster sugar
2 tsp palm sugar
½ green mango, finely
grated
2 shallots, finely chopped
1–2 bird's eye chillies,
coarsley chopped (optional)
6 tbsp lime juice

FOR SERVING
Handful of salad leaves
2 tbsp whole roasted cashew
nuts
Coriander leaves, for
garnish

TO PREPARE THE TUNA
Blend the drained tuna in a food processor on a low setting. Gradually add the breadcrumbs and a tablespoon of oil to the mixture and blend for a further 1–2 minutes, or until the mixture starts to get fluffy. Transfer the mixture onto a plate, then use your fingertips to mix it (like when making the topping for a crumble). Heat the remaining oil in a deep frying pan on a high heat until it is very hot (test it by dipping the tip of a wooden spoon or wooden chopstick into the oil; if the oil bubbles, it's ready). Gently drop the mixture into the oil, using a wooden spoon to gently move the mixture so that it's loosely held together. Fry for a few minutes each side or until golden brown, then remove to a paper towel and set aside.

TO PREPARE THE DRESSING
Mix the fish sauce, caster sugar and palm sugar in a small bowl. If the palm sugar is still lumpy, heat the mixture in a microwave for 20–30 seconds on full power to melt it. Add the green mango, as well as the shallots, the chilli if you're using it, and the lime juice, then mix well.

TO SERVE
Place the salad leaves onto a serving plate and lay the crispy tuna over the top. Sprinkle on the coriander leaves and cashew nuts, and serve with the mango dressing on the side.

ONE-DISH MEALS

Noodles and fried rice are regularly consumed in Thailand as one-dish meals. These dishes involve noodles or rice cooked and seasoned with a sauce, protein and vegetables. I suppose it's the Thai equivalent to Italian pastas and risottos. There's an enormous variety of noodle and fried rice dishes in Thailand, but I have chosen to share just a few delicious dishes here that are quick and easy to make.

PAD THAI WITH KING PRAWNS

Phat Thai kung sot ผัดไทยกุ้งสด

Pad Thai is thought to have been introduced to Thailand in the late 1930s or early 1940s, during the Second World War. A shortage of rice meant that the government wanted to reduce domestic consumption, so the prime minister launched a national competition to devise a noodle dish – and this is how the award winning stir-fried noodles became famous. The government encouraged street food sellers and restaurants throughout the country to sell Pad Thai in the hope that more rice would therefore be available for export, to bring in much-needed income for the country's struggling economy. Since then the dish has become phenomenally popular across Thailand and around the world. The dish got the 'Pad Thai' moniker later, as part of a campaign to promote Thai nationalism and centralisation.

Although the list of ingredients might seem intimidating, putting the dish together is relatively straightforward. The most important key to its success is the texture of the noodles: make sure there isn't too much liquid in the wok, as it will make the noodles mushy. If this happens, turn up the heat for a while and then reduce again to medium. You'll also need to work the wok relatively quickly to avoid overcooking.

A good Pad Thai should balance the sweetness of the palm sugar, the gentle sourness of the tamarind juice and the saltiness of the fish sauce. Feel free to adjust the levels of these ingredients to suit your personal taste.

Prep time
25 mins

Cooking time
10 mins

Serves
4

For the best results, toast the peanuts in a dry frying pan for five minutes or until they're golden brown, and leave them to cool slightly before chopping them up. This adds a gorgeous toasty flavour to the dish. You can also substitute them with cashew nuts if you prefer.

Serve this dish with freshly toasted peanuts, ground dried chilli, a fresh wedge of lime, bean sprouts and a banana flower – generally available in Asian shops – on the side. The ingredients listed below will give you an idea of how Thais enjoy this dish at home. If you can get all of them, great; but don't worry if you can't, as – depending on where you are – they can be hard to come by outside Thailand. It's not the end of the world if you can't get them; you'll still be able to create a fantastic plate of noodles. As long as the overall flavour is good, you'll be assured of a happy stomach!

Top tip

To save time, you can make up a batch of Pad Thai sauce and keep it in the fridge (it should last for up to three months), or freeze it as you might any other stock or sauce. (This tip is also followed by most restaurants and even posh hotels.) For the recipe, see p157. Once the sauce is ready, it's just a matter of adding it to the other ingredients.

Phat Thai kung sot   ผัดไทยกุ้งสด

FOR THE STIR-FRY

300 g dry Thai rice noodles

450 g raw king prawns, cleaned,
(peeled if preferred) and deveined

6 tbsp light-flavoured oil

5 gloves garlic, crushed

3 shallots, finely sliced

(optional) 60 g extra-firm tofu,
cut into cubes

(Optional) 2 tbsp preserved turnip
(*hua chai po*)

3 medium free-range eggs

80 g fresh bean sprouts

40 g Chinese chives (garlic
chives), or normal chives or spring
onions, chopped into 2.5 cm pieces

FOR THE SAUCE

6 tbsp tamarind sauce

6 tbsp palm sugar

6 tbsp fish sauce

2 tbsp white vinegar

Pinch of salt

Soak the dried noodles in lukewarm water at room temperature for 20 minutes, or follow the package instructions.

In a medium frying pan or wok, briefly fry the prawns in 2 tablespoons of oil for 1–2 minutes, being careful not to overcook them, then remove from the pan and set aside. Many Thai people like to cook king prawns with the shells on, as it helps to hold in the flavour and keep the prawns moist; you can use either peeled or unpeeled. In the same pan, heat the remaining oil over medium heat, then add the garlic and shallots. Fry for 1–2 minutes, until the shallots have softened. Add the tofu and turnip (if using), and stir-fry until they start to brown.

Drain the noodles well and then add them to the wok. Add all the sauce ingredients, and keep stirring gently to stop the noodles sticking to the wok.

Move the noodles to one side of the wok and crack the eggs into the other side. Stir the eggs as if you're scrambling them, until they have a slightly creamy texture but are not completely cooked. Fold the noodles into the eggs and stir them together, then add the beansprouts and Chinese chives. Check that the noodles are cooked. If they aren't, gradually add a little water until they are.

Add the cooked prawns. Stir quickly. Transfer the pad thai onto a serving plate and sprinkle with the peanuts. Serve with bean sprouts, fresh wedges of lime, ground dried chilli and a banana flower on the side.

STIR-FRIED RICE NOODLES WITH BEEF

Phat si oi nuea   ผัดซีอิ๊วเนื้อ

This stir-fried noodle dish is really an express meal, although I have seen many people enjoying it in restaurants outside Thailand as a side dish instead of plain rice. For this recipe, I typically use the pre-cooked fine rice vermicelli noodles available from most supermarkets. Since these have already been cooked, they don't need to be soaked in water before cooking. You can also use another meat of your choice, such as pork, chicken or seafood, with this dish. Thais serve this dish with a selection of condiments, such as chilli oil, vinegar, coriander and cucumber.

Prep time
10 mins

Cooking time
5 mins

Serves
4

6 tbsp light-flavoured oil
1 medium onion, finely sliced
4 garlic cloves, crushed
250 g lean beef, sliced
4 medium free-range eggs
120 g Chinese broccoli (*kai lan*) or broccoli, cut into 2.5 cm pieces
1 medium carrot, sliced into thin discs
550 g pre-cooked rice vermicelli noodles (or 300 g dry weight noodles, soaked in warm water for 10–15 minutes or according to instructions)
5–6 tbsp light soy sauce
2 tbsp oyster sauce
1 tbsp dark soy sauce
Pinch of caster sugar
Black pepper

Heat the oil in a wok and then add the onion and garlic. Fry for 30 seconds to 1 minute. Add the beef, and fry, stirring, until it's medium-rare.

Push the beef to one side of the wok, and then crack the eggs into it. Scramble them by stirring quickly.

Add the Chinese broccoli and carrot, and continue to stir for 3–5 more minutes. Add the noodles, and stir until all the ingredients are cooked. (Add a little water if the wok is getting too dry.) Season with the soy sauces, the oyster sauce and sugar.

Crack some black pepper over the noodles, and then serve.

RICE CONGEE WITH PORK DUMPLINGS AND GINGER

Chok mu   โจ๊กหมู

The idea of a savoury porridge might seem strange to many of you, but believe me, you will be blown away by its mild but flavourful taste. It's an incredibly light and cosy dish.

Rice congee originated as a food for times of hardship, to stretch the rice ration – by adding more water than usual and cooking until the rice disintegrates. *Chok* (pronounced 'joke') is typically served with chopped spring onion, ground white pepper, crunchy fried garlic, finely sliced fresh ginger and extra table seasonings.

Many Thais like to eat their congee with a raw egg, cracked into the hot congee before serving so that it cooks slightly. I like it with a soft-boiled egg. For me (as well as many Thai kids), this is the breakfast and the midnight feast I grew up with. It is what I crave when I have a cold, as it is so comforting. Try it, and you'll understand why. Feel free to divide these ingredients for one or two people or multiply to serve a bigger group.

Prep time
5 mins

Cooking time
15–20 mins

Serves
4

FOR THE CONGEE
400 g uncooked jasmine rice
1.5 l vegetable stock or water
4 tbsp light soy sauce

FOR THE PORK DUMPLINGS
500 g minced pork
2 garlic cloves, crushed
3 coriander roots or coriander stalks
2 tbsp light soy sauce
1 tbsp fish sauce
1 tbsp oyster sauce

FOR THE OPTIONAL TOPPING
2 tbsp light-flavoured oil
3 garlic cloves, coarsely chopped
4 medium free-range eggs, cooked for
7–8 minutes in freshly boiled water
until soft-boiled and then peeled
2–3 chunks fresh ginger, peeled and
finely sliced
2 tbsp spring onion, finely chopped
Handful of coriander, roughly chopped
Pinch of ground white pepper

Use a blender or food processor to blend the uncooked rice for about 30 seconds to a minute, until you achieve a nearly smooth texture. Add the rice to a large pot with the vegetable stock or water, and bring to the boil. Turn down the heat to medium-low, and let it simmer for 10 minutes.

While the rice is cooking, prepare the pork dumplings. In a food processor, combine the minced pork with the garlic, coriander root, soy sauce, fish sauce and oyster sauce and blend until smooth. To make the dumplings, form the mixture into balls about 2.5 cm in diameter, using your hands. Set aside.

To make the crispy fried garlic topping, heat the oil in a small frying pan and then fry the chopped garlic for 2 minutes until golden brown. Transfer to a small serving bowl.

When the rice is cooked, add the dumplings and bring to the boil. Cook for 2–3 minutes, until the pork turns opaque and is cooked through. Season the congee with the light soy sauce.

Serve the congee topped with a soft-boiled egg per person and a little ginger, spring onion, coriander, a sprinkling of white pepper, and the crispy fried garlic. You can put extra seasonings such as fish sauce and vinegar on the table, for people to add to their taste.

NOODLES WITH CHICKEN IN GRAVY

Rat na kai   ราดหน้าไก่

This is another variant on a Thai street food dish, and you can use any meat or seafood, or use more vegetables and firm tofu for a veggie version. The dish is often served with a selection of condiments, such as ground dried chilli, rice vinegar, sugar and fish sauce, so you can adjust the flavour at the table to suit your taste.

Prep time
10 mins

Cooking time
7 mins

Serves
4

FOR THE NOODLES
400 g pre-cooked rice noodles, or 200 g dry noodles (soaked in warm water for 10-15 mins or according to instructions)
4-5 tbsp light-flavoured oil
2 tbsp dark soy sauce

FOR THE GRAVY
2 tbsp cooking oil
3-4 garlic cloves, crushed
450 g chicken breasts (about 3 fillets), finely sliced
200 g Chinese broccoli (*kai lan*) or broccoli, cut into 2.5 cm pieces
2 medium carrots, finely sliced
800 ml chicken stock or water
4 tbsp light soy sauce
1 tbsp yellow bean paste (optional)
Pinch of sugar
4 tbsp room-temperature water
2 tbsp tapioca flour

Heat 4-5 tablespoons of oil in a wok over high heat and stir-fry the noodles with the dark soy sauce for 2-3 minutes or until al dente. Add a few tablespoons of water while cooking if the mixture is too solid. Remove the wok from the heat, transfer the noodles to a serving plate and set to the side.

In the same wok, add 2 tablespoons of oil and fry the garlic over medium heat for about 30 seconds. Add the chicken and cook for about 1 minute, before adding the broccoli and carrots.

Add the chicken stock, soy sauce, yellow bean paste (if using) and sugar. Bring to the boil and simmer for 2-3 minutes.

In a small cup or bowl, mix the tapioca flour and water, stirring well until the flour has thoroughly dissolved and the mixture has become smooth. Gradually pour the mixture into the wok, and stir continuously for a minute until the sauce becomes sticky.

Pour the gravy over the noodles in a serving dish, and serve with condiments.

RAILWAY CHICKEN FRIED RICE

Khao phat rot fai ข้าวผัดรถไฟ

Fried rice is very common in Thailand, but this particular type has its roots in the glorious past. It used to be sold on the old-fashioned open-air steam trains that ran up and down the country. Independent traders would hop on and off the trains at every station to sell refreshments, snacks and hot food – including fried rice. Hence the name 'railway fried rice'. This dish might not look as pretty as other, fancier dishes, but it's an honest dish that won't disappoint you. It works perfectly as an express meal or as a side dish.

The trick is to use cold steamed jasmine rice, as the grains of rice hold their shape better than freshly cooked rice. This dish is perfect for using up leftovers from the day before.

Prep time
10 mins

Cooking time
5–10 mins

Serves
4

2 tbsp light-flavoured oil
½ medium onion, finely sliced
2 garlic cloves, crushed
400 g chicken breast (approx. 2 breast fillets), finely sliced
2 free-range eggs
500 g cooked white rice (preferably cold jasmine rice)
150 g Chinese broccoli (*kai lan*) or broccoli, chopped into 2.5 cm pieces
3–4 medium tomatoes, sliced
2 tbsp light soy sauce
1 tbsp oyster sauce
1 tbsp dark soy sauce
1 tsp ground white or black pepper

In a large frying pan or wok, heat the cooking oil until very hot. Add the onion and garlic and stir-fry until the onion is soft.

Add the chicken, and cook, stirring occasionally, for a few minutes or until the chicken is almost cooked (it will change from pink to white).

Use a spatula to move all the ingredients in the wok to one side, then crack the eggs into the other side. Stir them quickly until you get scrambled eggs.

Add the rice, broccoli, tomatoes and all the seasonings. Stir quickly until the broccoli is well cooked and the rice is properly mixed with the other ingredients.

USE IT AGAIN AND AGAIN

Today, most Thai home cooks generally buy pre-made curry pastes and sauces, but few things are as satisfying as making them from scratch. Doing it yourself not only makes the sauces and pastes tastes fresher, but it means you also know exactly what's gone into them. And by making your own pastes and sauces every once in a while, you'll have these key Thai ingredients at your fingertips, ready whenever you want them. The curry pastes and sauces will keep for several weeks in a sterilised, airtight jar in the fridge, or you can freeze them, will which give you months of fine cooking!

GREEN CURRY PASTE

Phrik kaeng khiao wan   พริกแกงเขียวหวาน

1 tbsp coriander seeds

1 tsp cumin seeds

2 stalks lemongrass, cut into 2.5 cm pieces

1 medium galangal, sliced into ½ cm pieces

10-15 fresh green bird's eye chillies, deseeded

10-15 coriander roots

8 garlic cloves, chopped

4 shallots, roughly chopped

½ tsp zest of a kaffir lime

4 tbsp light-flavoured oil

2 tsp salt

1 tsp shrimp paste (omit for vegan)

In a small frying pan, toss the coriander and cumin seeds on a low heat for a few minutes until they begin to release their aromas. Remove from the heat and set aside.

In a pestle and mortar, or in a blender or food processor on a medium setting, pound/blitz the lemongrass and galangal, then add in the tossed coriander seeds and cumin seeds and the chillies, coriander roots, garlic, shallots and lime zest. During the blending process, add the oil to the mixture.

Season with the salt and shrimp paste, and continue to blend until smooth.

RED CURRY PASTE

Phrik kaeng phet   พริกแกงเผ็ด

2 stalks lemongrass, cut into 2.5 cm pieces

1 medium galangal, sliced into ½ cm pieces

10-15 dried red chillies, deseeded

10-15 coriander roots

8 garlic cloves, chopped

4 shallots, chopped

½ tsp zest of a kaffir lime

4 tbsp light-flavoured oil

2 tsp salt

1 tsp shrimp paste (omit for vegan)

Pound all the ingredients in a pestle and mortar, or blitz in a blender or food processor, starting with the lemongrass and galangal and then adding the chillies, coriander roots, garlic, shallots and lime zest. Add the oil during the blending process.

Season with the salt and shrimp paste, and continue to blend until you have a smooth paste.

PANANG CURRY PASTE

Phrik kaeng pha neang   พริกแกงพะแนง

2 tbsp coriander seeds

2 tsp cumin seeds

2 stalks lemongrass, cut into 2.5 cm pieces

1 medium galangal, sliced into ½ cm pieces

10-15 dried red chillies, deseeded

10-15 coriander roots

15 garlic cloves, chopped

8 shallots, chopped

½ tsp zest of a kaffir lime

4 tbsp light-flavoured oil

2 tsp salt

1 tsp shrimp paste (omit for vegan)

In a small frying pan, toss the coriander and cumin seeds on a low heat for a few minutes, until they begin to release their aromas. Remove from the heat and set to the side.

Pound all the ingredients in a pestle and mortar, or blitz in a blender or food processor, starting with the lemongrass and galangal and then adding the chillies, tossed coriander seeds and cumin seeds, coriander roots, garlic, shallots and lime zest. Add the oil during the blending process.

Season with the salt and shrimp paste, and continue to blend until you have a smooth paste.

MASSAMAN CURRY PASTE

Phrik kaeng massaman   พริกแกงมัสมั่น

10-15 coriander roots

4 shallots, chopped

5-6 dry long red chillies, soaked in water
for 10-15 minutes and then deseeded

8 garlic cloves, chopped

2 stalks lemongrass, cut into 2.5 cm pieces

3 cinnamon sticks

1 medium galangal, sliced into ½ cm pieces

5 whole cloves

3 whole nutmeg

2 tbsp sunflower oil

1 tbsp coriander seeds

1 tsp cumin seeds

1 tsp whole or ground black pepper

1 tsp salt

1 tsp shrimp paste (omit for vegan version)

In a dry medium-sized frying pan, toast all the spice ingredients - everything except the oil, salt and shrimp paste - for a few minutes to release their aromas.

Transfer the spices and the rest of the ingredients to a pestle and mortar or food processor, and pound/blend until the mixture forms a rough paste. Add the oil during the process, to blend the ingredients.

Season with the salt and shrimp paste, and continue to blend until you have a smooth paste.

YELLOW CURRY PASTE

Phrik kaeng lueang   พริกแกงเหลือง

2 dried red chillies, washed and deseeded

4-5 garlic cloves, peeled and halved

2 pieces galangal root, each 2.5 cm long

2 pieces fresh turmeric, each 2.5 cm long
(or 4 tsp ground turmeric)

2 shallots, peeled and halved

1 tsp shrimp paste (omit for vegan version)

2 tbsp water

Toast all the ingredients in a dry wok or frying pan for a few minutes until they're slightly golden and fragrant.

Transfer the mixture, along with 1-2 tbsp of water, to a pestle and mortar or blender, and pound/blend for 2-3 minutes until you have a smooth paste.

PAD THAI SAUCE

Nam sot phat Thai น้ำซอสผัดไทย

> **Top tip**
>
> Some people add shallots and peanuts when making this sauce, but I would recommend leaving them out at this stage, because the sauce will keep longer without them. You can add them when you actually cook the final Pad Thai dish. Use about 2-3 tablespoons of this sauce for each person you're cooking for.

250 g palm sugar
120 ml water
240 ml fish sauce
240 ml tamarind sauce
½ tbsp chilli powder

Combine the sugar and the water in a deep non-stick saucepan, and cook over a low heat until the sugar has dissolved.

Add the fish sauce, tamarind sauce and the chilli. Bring to the boil, and then reduce the heat. Cook, stirring gently every few minutes until the sauce has reduced and become sticky.

SPICY DIPPING SAUCE FOR SEAFOOD

Nam chim ta le น้ำจิ้มทะเล

10 garlic cloves, peeled
10 bird's eye chillies, deseeded if preferred
6 tbsp fish sauce
6 tbsp lime juice
2 tbsp garlic pickle brine or brine from a jar of green olives
2 tbsp caster sugar or honey

Blend the garlic and chilli in a food processor or blender on a low setting for about 30 seconds. Add the fish sauce, lime juice, garlic brine and sugar. Stir well until the sugar has dissolved.

Once cooled, store in a sterilised air-tight bottle and keep in the fridge, as you would any salad dressing.

CUCUMBER RELISH

Achat อาจาด

6 tbsp white vinegar
6 tbsp palm sugar
2 tbsp water
Pinch of salt
½ cucumber, chopped into small cubes
1 shallot, peeled and finely chopped
1 fresh long chilli
Small handful of coriander

In a small saucepan, combine the vinegar, sugar, water and salt. Heat over a medium flame until the sugar has dissolved.

Remove from the heat and let the liquid cool completely. Add the cucumber, shallot, chilli and coriander, and mix through. This relish can be served right away or can be kept in the fridge for a few days.

PEANUT SATAY SAUCE

Nam chim sa te น้ำจิ้มสะเต๊ะ

1 tbsp red curry paste (p. 154)
250 ml coconut milk
120 ml water
200 g unsalted roasted peanuts, ground (smooth peanut butter is an acceptable substitute)
2 tbsp palm sugar
1 tbsp tamarind sauce
Pinch of salt

In a medium-sized saucepan over a low heat, combine the red curry paste with a few tablespoons of coconut milk, and stir until the fat separates from the milk.

Add the rest of the coconut milk and the water, and season with the peanuts, sugar, tamarind sauce and salt. Continue cooking on a low heat, stirring constantly, for 2-3 minutes, until you can see a layer of fat forming on the top. Let the sauce cool before serving.

TOASTED GROUND RICE

Khao Khua ข้าวคั่ว

250 g glutinous rice or Thai jasmine rice

(Optional) 1 slice (5 mm thick) galangal, or ½ stalk lemongrass, finely sliced

Toss the rice grains and the galangal or lemongrass in a clean, dry, medium-sized frying pan on a low heat.

Stir constantly until the rice turns golden brown (this should take about 3-5 minutes).

Remove from the heat and leave to cool, then grind in a pestle and mortar, or blend in a food processor for 30 seconds to 1 minute.

STOCKS

Nam sup   น้ำซุป

Top tip

These homemade stocks (**nam sup**, น้ำซุป) can be used for cooking as a flavourful replacement for water in many recipes. Put the cooled stock in an airtight container or freezer bag designed for liquid, and store in the freezer for up to six months.

CHICKEN STOCK   Nam sup kai   น้ำซุปไก่

3 l cold water
500 g raw or cooked chicken carcasses, chopped into manageable pieces
2 medium carrots, roughly chopped
3 sticks celery, roughly chopped
1 medium onion, roughly chopped
5 garlic cloves, peeled and crushed
Pinch of freshly ground black pepper
Pinch of salt

Add the chicken carcasses to a large pot together with the garlic, celery, carrot, onion, black pepper and salt. Add the water and bring to the boil, and cook for 5-10 minutes. Turn the heat down, cover with a lid and simmer for at least 2 hours. You can also use a slow cooker on the low setting for 6-8 hours.

I put the slow cooker on in the morning before leaving for work, and the stock will then be ready to be used by the time I get home.

PORK STOCK   Nam sup kra duk mu   น้ำซุปกระดูกหมู

3 l cold water
500 g raw pork ribs or bones, chopped into manageable pieces
2 medium carrots, roughly chopped
3 sticks celery, roughly chopped
1 medium onion, roughly chopped
5 garlic cloves, unpeeled and crushed
Pinch of freshly ground black pepper
Pinch of salt

Add the pork ribs to a large pot together with the garlic, celery, carrot, onion, black pepper and salt. Add the water and bring to the boil, cooking for 5-10 minutes. Turn the heat down, cover with a lid and simmer for at least 2 hours.

You can also use a slow cooker on the low setting for 6-8 hours.

MENU IDEAS

As mentioned at the beginning of this book, Thai food is all about sharing and celebrating the harmony of textures and balance of flavour. In case you need some inspiration for your Thai meals, here are some examples of what a typical Thai meal looks like-whether cooking for a large party, hosting a few close friends or just making a week night meal for family. I hope you enjoy cooking them!

CLASSIC THAI MEAL

Serve all dishes together, to be eaten in a Thai sharing style.

Thai BBQ Pork (p.76)
Spicy Minced Chicken Salad with Toasted Ground Rice (p.132)
Spicy Green Papaya Salad (p.126)
Sticky rice (p.42)

PERFECT THAI-STYLE SUMMER BBQ

Pick any one of these dishes to serve alongside your usual selections, or make the whole lot!

Thai Prawn Cakes (p.50)
Chicken Satay (p.49)
Sweet Tomato and Minced Pork Relish (p.49)
served with carrots and cucumber sticks
Thai BBQ Pork (p.76)
Spicy Green Papaya Salad (p.126)
Sticky rice (p.42)

ULTIMATE THAI DINNER PARTY

Show off to your guests with this delicious fuss-free meal. Easy to cook, a short list of ingredients and you can prepare most of them in advance.

MENU A

Thai Prawn Cakes (p.50)
Massaman Curry with Chicken (p.91)
Jasmine, brown or sticky rice (p.40,41,42)
Mixed Vegetables in Oyster Sauce (p.114)
(Dessert suggestion: mango sorbet)

ULTIMATE THAI DINNER PARTY

MENU B

Aromatic Chicken Coconut Soup (p.63)
Roasted Duck in Tamarind Sauce, served with steamed broccoli (p.93)
Mixed Vegetables in Oyster Sauce (p.114)
Jasmine rice (p.40)
(Dessert suggestion: coconut ice cream)

SEAFOOD EXTRAVAGANZA

Especially selected for seafood fanatics.

MENU A

Fishy Curry Cupcakes (p.48)
Steamed Sea Bass with Ginger and Spring Onion (p.100)
Stir-fried Clams with Chilli Paste and Thai Sweet Basil (p.109)
Aubergine with Thai Sweet Basil (p.112)
Jasmine or brown rice (p.40,41)

MENU B

Creamy King Prawn Tom Yum Soup (p.58)
Steamed Mussels with Thai Herbs (p.102) and Spicy Dipping Sauce for Seafood (p.157)
Mixed Seafood Stir-fried with Curry Powder (p.106)
Aubergine with Thai Sweet Basil (p.112)
Jasmine or brown rice (p.40,41)

MENU C

Crispy Squid with Garlic and Pepper (p.46)
Stir-fried Clams with Chilli Paste and Thai Sweet Basil (p.102)
Steamed King Prawns with Herb-infused Glass Noodles (p.100)
Mixed Vegetables in Oyster Sauce (p.114)
Jasmine or brown rice (p.40,41)

VEGGIE FEAST

Especially selected for fun-loving vegetarians!

MENU A

Aubergine with Thai Sweet Basil (p.112)
Southern-style Yellow Curry with Pineapple (p.118)
Jasmine rice (p.40)
Mixed Vegetables in Oyster Sauce (p.114)

MENU B

Northern-style Chargrilled Chilli Relish (p.71)
Duck Eggs with a Shallot and Tamarind Sauce (p.122)
Jasmine rice (p.40)
(Suggested side dish: steamed broccoli)

COSY NIGHT-IN TREATS

These are hassle-free dinner ideas, ideal for weeknights – these dishes take less than 20 minutes and are both delicious and satisfying.

Monday: Stir-fried Mixed Seafood with Curry Powder, jasmine rice (p.109,40)
Tuesday: Chicken with Ginger and Spring Onions, jasmine rice (p.88,40)
Wednesday: Green Curry with Chicken, jasmine rice (p.86,40)
Thursday: Stir-fried Beef in Oyster Sauce, jasmine rice (p.81,40)
Friday: Dry Red Curry with Salmon, jasmine rice (p.105,40)

EXPRESS LUNCHES

These dishes take less than 15 minutes to cook from scratch and are perfect for a weekend lunch.

Pork in Garlic and Pepper, jasmine rice (p.78,40)
Stir-fried Rice Noodles with Beef (p.144)
Stir-fried Pork with Holy Basil, jasmine rice (p.80,40)
King Prawns with Asparagus, jasmine rice (p.99,40)
Thai Omelette with Garlic and Mushrooms (p.116,40)

FEELING PECKISH

Nice and quick dishes, perfect for snacking or as nibbles for a party.

Crispy Squid with Garlic and Pepper (p.46)
Chargrilled Chilli and Mackerel Relish (p.70)
Northern-style Chargrilled Chilli Relish (p.71)
Glass Noodle and King Prawn Salad (p.128)
Crispy Tuna Salad with Green Mango Dressing (p.136)
Chargrilled Aubergine with Toasted Coconut Salad (p.134)

HEALTHY SECRETS

Fresh and packed with nutrition.

Chargrilled Chilli and Mackerel Relish (p.70)
Northern-style Chargrilled Chilli Relish (p.71)
Sweet Tomato and Minced Pork Relish (p.68)
Glass Noodle and King Prawn Salad (p.128)
Salad with Garlic Pork, Lime and Fresh Mint (p.130)
Spicy Minced Chicken Salad with Toasted Ground Rice (p.132)
Steamed Sea Bass in Garlic and Lime Sauce (p.101)

CONVERSION TABLES

WEIGHT AND LENGTH CONVERSIONS

1 centimetre	1/3 inch approx.
2.5 centimetres	1 inch
10 grams	0.35 ounces
100 grams	3.5 ounces
250 grams	9 ounces, ½ pound approx.
500 grams	17.5 ounces, 1 pound approx.

VOLUME CONVERSIONS

1 teaspoon	5 millilitres
1 tablespoon	15 millilitres, 3 teaspoons
4 tablespoons	60 millilitres, ¼ cup, 2 fluid ounces
8 tablespoons	120 millilitres, ½ cup, 4 fluid ounces
100 millilitres	6 ½ tbsp, 0.4 cups, 3.4 fluid ounces
240 millilitres	1 cup, 8 fluid ounces, ½ US pint
500 millilitres	2 cups, 17 fluid ounces, 1 US pint
1 litre	1 quart, 4 cups, 2 US pints

TEMPERATURE CONVERSIONS

Celsius	Fahrenheit	Gas Mark	Terminology
140°C	275°F	1	Very cool/very slow
150°C	300°F	2	Cool/slow
165°C	325°F	3	Warm
180°C	350°F	4	Moderate
190°C	375°F	5	Moderate
200°C	400°F	6	Moderately hot
220°C	425°F	7	Hot
230°C	450°F	8	Hot
245°C	475°F	9	Very hot

NOTE ON TRANSLITERATION

Thai words in this book are transcribed based on the 1999 version of the Royal Thai General System of Transcription (RTGS), which is the official system published by the Royal Institute of Thailand.

Although this system does not completely reflect the pronunciation of a native Thai speaker, it will help a non-Thai reader to pronounce Thai words with reasonable accuracy. Note, however, that the *ph* sound is pronounced like the English *p*, and *th* like a *t*. The only exceptions in this book are words whose spellings are already widely used in English, such as *larb* or pad thai.

SOURCES AND FURTHER READING

Blumenthal, Mark, ed., *Herbal Medicine: Expanded Commission E Monographs*, American Botanical Council, 2000

Evenson, Robert E., Robert W. Herdt and Mahabub Hossain, *Rice Research in Asia: Progress and Priorities*, Wallingford, Oxon, 1996

Freer, Amelia, *Eat. Nourish. Glow.*, London, 2015

'Ginger', US National Library of Medicine, https://nccih.nih.gov/health/ginger, accessed 17 October 2013

Hmom Rachawong Yai Suwapan Sanitwong Na Ayuthaya, *The Rice of Siam*, Bangkok, 1988

Hom, Ken, *Simple Thai Cookery*, London, 2006

Moncel, Bethany, '*What Is Oyster Sauce?*', www.thespruce.com, accessed 12 May 2017

'Oven Temperature Conversion', www.inspiredtaste.net/23326/oven-temperature-conversion, accessed 30 August 2017

Punyarathbandhu, Leela, *Simple Thai Food*, Berkeley, CA, 2014

Puri, Harbans Singh, *Rasayana: Ayurvedic Herbs for Longevity and Rejuvenation*, Boca Raton, FL, 2002, pp. 272–80

Thompson, David, *Thai Food*, London, 2013

Index

ACKNOWLEDGEMENTS

Who would have thought that a simple conversation in front of the TV in my living room with Adam Newman, who happened to be staying at my house, would spark the idea of documenting my recipes. Although he probably now has no memory of our chat, I thank him for inspiring me to start this journey.

I thank my hero dad, my mum, my sister, my brother, my grandma and all my family, who have been the wind beneath my wings. I would also like to thank my husband and my cheeky children, Maia and Isaac, for believing in me.

A big thank you to Taran Wilkhu for the beautiful photographs shot in the UK and for being instrumental in generally ensuring this book happened. I thank my special friend Namthip, for her efforts to make sure the photo shoot in Thailand happened; and thank you to Sursart, for the amazing photographs shot there.

Thank you to Aimee Selby for her patience in bringing my English up to standard, and to Ben Sumner for being my book mentor. I also want to thank everyone who tested my recipes.

Thank you to the 'Priao Jai Gang', my best friends from Thammasat University, and to all my friends outside Thailand for being my eating partners in crime.

I'm also thankful to my favourite chefs, David Thompson and Jamie Oliver, whose passions for food inspired me personally while writing this book.

Finally, thank you to all the farmers, cooks, street food vendors, market stall holders and great restaurants in Thailand for making Thailand arguably the world's greatest food nation!

Published in the United Kingdom by
The Big Cheeks Publishing Ltd.
155 Sydenham Park Road
London SE26 4LP

Hard cover ISBN:978-1-9999392-0-5
eBook ISBN:978-1-9999392-1-2

Printed by
Basildon Printing Company Limited

Design by
Benji Roebuck

Layout by
Sirilak Wichianpaisan

Photography by
In Thailand: Surasart Areear ifeelgoodphotographer.com
In United Kingdom: Taran Wilkhu

Food stylist
Namthip Yodpanyadee

Editor
Aimee Selby

ABOUT THE AUTHOR

Sirilak was born and raised in Phitsanulok, Thailand. Her nickname is Salee and that's how she is known among her friends and family. She was educated locally until the age of eighteen, when she went to Thammasat University in Bangkok and received her Bachelor's degree in journalism and mass communication. During her studies, she had the rare opportunity of an internship as a junior producer at the BBC World Service in Bangkok and London. After finishing university, Salee moved to London and landed a job at the Royal Thai Embassy. Later, she worked as a freelance journalist, writing for AmThai newspaper. Salee now works for a commercial insurance company in the city of London.

While living far away from the place of her birth, being able to enjoy and share the flavours that she loves with friends and family helps Salee stay connected to her roots. This is what inspired this book – her wish to share her passion with as many food lovers as possible wherever they are.